GET A LIFE !

SKINT to mint

Sarah Modlock

Hodder Arnold

A MEMBER OF THE HODDER HEADLINE GROUP

Orders: Please contact Bookpoint Ltd, 130 Milton Park, Abingdon, Oxon, OX14 4SB.
Telephone: (44) 01235 827720, Fax: (44) 01235 400454. Lines are open from 9.00 to 17.00, Monday
to Saturday, with a 24-hour message answering service. You can also order through our website
www.hoddereducation.com

British Library Cataloguing in Publication Data
A catalogue record for this title is available from the British Library.

ISBN-10: 0 340 908025
ISBN-13: 9 780340 908020

First published   2006
Impression number   10 9 8 7 6 5 4 3 2 1
Year   2008   2007   2006

Typeset by Pantek Arts Ltd, Maidstone, Kent.
Printed in Great Britain for Hodder Arnold, a division of Hodder Headline,
338 Euston Road, London, NW1 3BH, by Bath Press, Bath.

The publisher has used its best endeavours to ensure that the URLs for external websites referred to in
this book are correct and active at the time of going to press. However, the publisher and the author
have no responsibility for the websites and can make no guarantee that a site will remain live or that
the content will remain relevant, decent or appropriate.

Hodder Headline's policy is to use papers that are natural, renewable and recyclable products and made
from wood grown in sustainable forests. The logging and manufacturing processes are expected to
conform to the environmental regulations of the country of origin.

Every effort has been made to trace copyright for material used in this book. The authors and
publishers would be happy to make arrangements with any holder of copyright whom it has not been
possible to trace successfully by the time of going to press.

CONTENTS

DEDICATION

For my inspirational, talented, beautiful mother Lilian.

INTRODUCTION

Welcome to *Skint to Mint*. I'm Sarah Modlock, your money coach over the 100 days as you progress through the book.

If you think you are 'no good with money' then you are not alone. Considering how essential money is to our lives, there is no dedicated 'personal finance' lesson at school and most of us rely on our parents as examples when it comes to understanding income, bills and savings. From the moment you open your first bank account, earn your first pay cheque or take on a student loan, you are engaging in the big world of money. But there is no magic wand to bless you with the knowledge and understanding needed to successfully manage your cash.

How many people do you know who absolutely love managing money? Think carefully. I don't just mean the occasional smarty-pants who boasts about their swish new credit card. I can think of about three offhand: Donald Trump, the Governor of the Bank of England and my brother Michael. Most of us mere mortals prefer to spend time living life rather than counting pennies. Unfortunately, it's not that simple. Opting out of financial responsibility will lead, sooner or later, to a miserable life. Whether you are under-saving, over-spending or just ignoring bank statements, you can end up unable to afford the lifestyle you want, feeling constantly anxious about your cash or dealing with debt.

It's important not to feel overwhelmed by the idea that your finances are worse than everyone else's. They are almost certainly not. But money is a personal thing and even close friends will rarely discuss financial blips or worries, creating the impression that you are struggling alone.

If you have been burying your head in the sand, or are just at a loss over how to get your money on track, then this book will provide everything you need – apart from a big pile of cash. In just 100 days you will:

◆ Have a very clear idea of how your income balances with what you spend
◆ Know whether you are living within your means and what to do if you are not
◆ Be able to spot any unhelpful spending habits and learn how to avoid and change them
◆ Feel more confident about your cash and understand how it can be more liberating than credit
◆ Confront any debts you have, make them cheaper, put into action a plan to pay them off and avoid them in future
◆ Understand how credit and loans work and how to use them sensibly to your advantage
◆ Start saving for long-term and short-term goals and rainy days, using the best accounts
◆ Get to grips with a wide range of financial products from mortgages to investments and pensions
◆ Learn how to keep your credit record healthy and avoid identity theft
◆ Take control of your finances for good and realise that managing your money is not that hard after all.

Although I will be with you on every page of the book, each day has a clear activity and requires you to be proactive if you want to progress. Like anything new, there will be days when you feel inspired and others when it feels more challenging. Just remember that persevering through the tougher days will lead you to great and lasting results.

If you require more detailed information about any aspects covered in this book, if you have questions about something that is not included, or if you want to tell me about your success stories then I'd be delighted to hear from you. E-mail me at skinttomint@yahoo.co.uk. I won't be able to provide specific advice on your financial decisions but I can point you in the right direction for generic information and help.

Finally, look upon each day as being another inch closer to having the grown-up, worry-free money skills that will set you up for life. If I can do it, then you can.

CHAPTER 1

WHY YOUR
MONEY MATTERS

Being in debt and low on cash takes away flexibility and choice, not to mention fun. Losing control of your finances is something that doesn't usually happen overnight. It creeps up over time so that you hardly notice you're slipping further from the black and into the red. It may seem easier living from one pay day to the next and juggling loans and overdrafts, but if this goes on for months or years it becomes a lifestyle built around bad money habits. Even the bucket load of self-loathing you tip over yourself at the same time every month – when you've run out of cash but don't get paid for another ten days – doesn't snap you out of the vicious circle. Congratulations on taking this first step towards healthier finances.

There are so many ways to get more from your money. After all, you work hard to earn it, so make sure it works hard for you. If you're constantly giving yourself excuses about your finances, then these examples will sound familiar:

'I'll catch up and start getting straight next month when I get paid.'

Well it sounds great in theory but the reality is that by next pay day there's likely to be a whole host of new distractions, activities and other demands on your cash. To break the cycle of spending and debt, you need to plan further ahead, look closely at where your money's going and make some changes that will last.

'My credit card's fine – they're all the same anyway.'

With a couple of thousand cards available there's plenty of competition for your business and no excuse for sticking with the same card through good and bad. Switching financial products has never been so easy and simple. You can save money on everything from your credit card to your mobile phone bill, your holiday insurance to your mortgage.

WHY YOUR MONEY MATTERS

How to use this book

Skint to Mint is divided into 100 steps, and has been designed as a 100-day programme. However, quick turnarounds aren't always possible and some steps may take longer than a day – it's up to you to take as much time as you need for each step. But do try to read one step every day – if only to keep yourself motivated – you can then go back to focus on a particular step if you need to.

Activity

Keep a money diary

- Start by keeping a money diary for the next five days.

- Include absolutely everything you spend from your morning coffee to your evening meal.

- The results will be essential when you come to look at your budget and detox your finances.

You'll be surprised at how easy it is to start sorting your finances out. You really don't need anything more complicated than a little time and a few basic items to begin the detox and make great changes.

Activity

Your financial detox toolkit

Start by setting aside some quiet time alone – or with your partner if you're looking at joint finances – when you know you won't be interrupted, distracted or be too tired.

Gather the items and documents you need:

- several sheets of A4 lined paper

- pen

- highlighter pen

- your diary

- a simple calculator

plus:

- around six months of bank statements and credit card bills

- any other financial documents related to your regular finances, such as loan agreements.

TOP TIP

- Use whatever information you have and save statements and bills from now on. They come in useful for all sorts of financial planning.

The most essential requirement is honesty. If you can't be honest with yourself, who can you be honest with?

TOP TIP

◆ Aim to hang on to receipts and cash machine slips from now on – put them to one side in a box or envelope so that you can use them to check against bills and statements in the future. You'd be surprised how many errors are made.

If you've thrown away your bank statements, you should be able to get copies from your bank, although check whether they will charge for this. You should be able to get free access to back copies if you bank online.

'To fulfill a dream, to be allowed to sweat over lonely labor, to be given a chance to create, is the meat and potatoes of life. The money is the gravy.' Bette Davis, actress

WHY YOUR MONEY MATTERS

Banks are probably much more understanding than you think. This is mainly because they like to ensure they have a good chance of getting back any money you owe them. If you're struggling to live within your means or find yourself slipping into debt, then your bank is likely to want to help. But banks run out of sympathy if you bury your head in the sand and fail to reply to their letters or telephone calls. Don't fall into the trap of ignoring your finances – keep up to date and open every statement and bill when it arrives.

CASE STUDY

Clare never opened her bank statements because she kept a rough idea of her bank balance in her head and would only be worried if the cash machine stopped giving her money too far from pay day. When she did begin to slip into debt, it then became harder to contemplate turning the situation around and every bill and bank statement remained unopened because its contents were sure to spoil her day. The next items to start arriving in the post were letters from her bank and credit card issuer. In the past, these had often contained new information about her bank account or an offer to increase her credit limit so it was easy to dismiss these, unopened.

Activity

Sort your statements

- Open all your bank, credit card and store card statements and put them into date order.

- You may find that you have separate statements from your bank showing any quarterly or monthly fees that apply to your account.

- If most or all of your statements are unopened then this is a habit to change. Clare's situation shows how ignoring your financial paperwork can make a problem worse.

Now that your bills and statements are no longer scary, you can make good use of them.

Activity

Read your statements

- Tick off all the cheques from your cheque book that appear on the statement; do the same for any credits paid in and debit card items. If there are any entries you don't recognise then make a note of them and follow them up.

- Check that all your regular standing orders and direct debits are shown correctly on the statement. If you don't recognise any, then make a note to follow them up with your bank. It could be that you're paying for forgotten memberships or subscriptions. It's especially easy to ignore regular transfers for small amounts – but it all adds up.

- Note outstanding items: some items might not yet have appeared on your latest statement. For example, the bank may not yet have received recently issued cheques; recent credits might not yet have cleared with the bank.

Spotted a problem with your bank statement? If you believe an error's been made, contact your branch as soon as possible. This is best done in writing and you should keep a copy of your letter. Don't send back the original bank statement but send a copy if you want to point something out to them. The bank will investigate. If an error has occurred that's their fault, then they should correct it. If their error has resulted in bank charges being made or other deductions

TheBank 454 High Street Sometown ST14 YH6		Mr. A. J. Wells The Coach House Bath Road Sometown ST5 KT2
ACCOUNT NUMBER: 80562991 SORT CODE: 30-62-80		STATEMENT: 32 PAGE: 1 of 1
	CREDITS	DEBITS
Salary	£1200.00	
Those flowers for mum		£35.00
Massive credit card bill		£875.00
Those gorgeous shoes		£70.00
Forgotten membership of gym you never visited		£45.00

from your account, they should make good the mistake and re-credit the sums involved. If you're unhappy with their reply, then you should arrange an appointment to see someone in the branch or go direct to the bank to discuss the problem.

TOP TIP

- Hang onto receipts from cash machine withdrawals, credit card and debit card transactions and fill in your cheque counterfoils. Check these against your bank and credit card statements when they arrive and if you don't recognise a transaction advise your bank or credit card issuer immediately. Keep a note of any regular transactions that are automatically debited to your account.

WHY YOUR MONEY MATTERS

As we've discovered, one of the easiest ways to lose track of your day-to-day finances and cash flow is through never checking your balance, forgetting that cheques or direct debits are about to leave your account and failing to read statements. Banking online can help avoid these problems.

Did you know?

These days, almost every high-street bank and building society offers the chance to view your account on their online system, free of charge. In addition to keeping close tabs on your balance and being able to spot errors more quickly, you can pay bills, transfer cash and do many of the banking activities you normally arrange in a branch, including applying for savings accounts, loans and credit cards online. You can access your account day or night – you can pay bills in your pyjamas if that's your thing.

Activity
Take your account online

Talk to your bank and take your account online. This may take a few days to complete but start today and you'll be surprised how quickly you get the hang of it. If you don't have a computer at home, you may still find online access is useful via work or library computers.

FACT: Some online banks update information in real-time, while others do it daily. Many highlight imminent outgoing amounts from cheques, standing orders or direct debits so that you don't get carried away by thinking your balance is larger than you expected.

TOP TIP

- Although no online system can be completely safe, banks have a vested interest in making their customers feel comfortable about online banking, and take great steps to maintain a high level of security.
- In fact, the only really vulnerable area is your PIN and password. That's why it's so important to keep them safe. Provided you keep your password confidential and ensure that others can't see your PC screen when you sign on, internet banking is just as safe as any other form of banking.
- Take simple precautions such as clearing your browser's cache when you exit and if your browser has the ability to remember passwords and user names, consider disabling this function or always decline the option to save your bank password.
- If you access your account on a public computer, close the browser after use.

WHY YOUR MONEY MATTERS

Your notes

CHAPTER 2

BUDGET CLEANSE

Neglect and bad spending will give your finances indigestion. Before you start to make improvements you need to look carefully at what's going into – and coming out of – your finances. Today will help you see the big picture.

The key to managing your finances effectively and avoiding debt is to draw up a simple budget – and stick to it. The word budget may make you think of the dull facts and figures announced by the Chancellor of the Exchequer. He may keep tabs on the nation's money but your budget just involves balancing your books and making sure you only spend what you can afford. It will form the basis of all the good work you'll do to improve your finances and will be essential throughout many of the next steps.

> 'My problem is how to reconcile my net income with my gross habits.' Errol Flynn, actor

Activity
Start drawing up your budget

- Choose a time when you can have some peace and quiet and won't be distracted. If possible, sit at a table so you can spread things out.

- Start with a blank sheet of paper divided into two columns. In the first column, list details of your monthly income. Apart from your salary, this should include any benefits such as tax credits or child benefit. If you have joint finances, include your partner's salary (but then don't forget to include joint costs and debts as you complete the next steps).

- In the second column write down all your monthly outgoings. Unless you live like a hermit, this list will inevitably be longer than the other one. But don't panic. It's important to be completely honest about what you do with your cash and writing everything down to start with will help you spot any unnecessary spending.

- List essential commitments such as your mortgage or rent and council tax. Divide any essential bills you pay annually or quarterly into the cost per month. If you make monthly contributions to a savings account, life insurance policy or pension plan, then include them.

- Now add up the costs so you have a sub-total for essential spending.

INCOMINGS	OUTGOINGS
Salary	Mortgage/rent
Partner's salary	Building and
Benefits	contents
	insurance
	Utilities
	Council tax
	Car insurance
	MOT and servicing
	Car tax
	Credit cards
	Loans
	Pension
	Life insurance
SUB-TOTAL	SUB-TOTAL

Next comes everyday spending, which examines your more common monthly costs. This is where your money diary comes into its own. By now you should have a clear idea of how much you spend on day-to-day items such as food, toiletries, travel and the dozens of small items, which soon add up. You may have even surprised yourself with how much – or how little – you pay out in an average week.

Don't forget to include the following if they feature in your everyday spending:

◆ children and their day-to-day costs, clothes, toys, etc
◆ your passions – whatever they may be – clothes, gadgets, books, things that may not have come up in your money diary like trips to the hairdresser or regular beauty treatments.

Activity

Calculate your everyday spending

- Underneath the total for essential monthly spending, on your budget, record your everyday spending costs.

- To give you one monthly figure, add the week's costs together and times them by four to get a estimated monthly total.

- If your lifestyle was unusually quiet while keeping your money diary then add estimates, which will make your spending as realistic as possible.

- If you usually head to the pub or wine bar after work three times a week but only did it once during your money diary week, then record a figure that's closer to your usual spending.

- Of course, if you kept your money diary during an unusually wild week then you could round the figures down slightly. Remember that honesty is crucial so don't be tempted to fake it.

- Now add up the everyday spending costs for another sub-total.

It's very easy to forget occasional costs that may only come up once or twice a year but still have to be paid for.

Think about:

◆ holidays
◆ birthdays
◆ hen or stag nights or trips
◆ weddings
◆ christenings
◆ Christmas
◆ home improvements such as decorating, furniture or gardening
◆ dentist visits
◆ optician visits and costs of glasses, contact lenses and accessories.

Some of these may be hard to anticipate. Occasional spending may involve more pressure than other areas. Weddings, for example, are not always easy to predict and some can involve everything from the cost of a gift to extensive travel, cash for drinks and an overnight stay. It's also possible to spend a small fortune on hen and stag parties or trips. Again, these can involve a budget covering anything from a night in the pub to a week abroad and everything in between.

Avoid the pressure

It's incredibly hard to own up to being skint or to miss out on an event or trip that's talked about for years afterwards. But if you're honest about your limited budget, you might find that others are relieved, too. Big groups heading on big trips require excellent planning skills, and thinking ahead can help avoid unnecessary costs.

CASE STUDY

A group of 12 blokes spent a long stag weekend at the Munich Beer Festival. The best man booked plane tickets and a hotel room for the groom and himself, but by the time he sent the details round to the rest of the stags, the hotel was full and the flight prices had shot up. Not only did the boys resent spending beer money on the extra airfare, they were scattered in hotels over different parts of the city, which dented the group spirit a little as their taxis headed off in different directions every night. A bit of planning would have saved everyone money and helped morale.

Activity

Calculate your occasional spending

- Estimate some basic costs across the year.

- Then divide the amount by 12 to calculate the monthly sub-total for occasional spending.

- Remember, it's better to have some flexibility built into your budget than to get nasty surprises.

Activity

Reveal your completed budget

- Your efforts are already paying off as you add all three outgoing sub-totals in the right-hand column of your budget sheet to make a grand total.

- Then deduct this from your total monthly income.

- You'll now have a clear idea of whether your spending exceeds your income and by how much. With any luck, you'll be living within your means.

If you've money to spare, then you'll find everything you need in this book to increase any debt repayments, bump up your savings or put cash aside for a rainy day. Once you're in great financial shape and debt free, there's the option of making more of your money over the longer term through investments.

If you're not living within your means, then it's time to look more closely at where your money goes and identify areas where you can cut back or make sacrifices. Unless you're living a champagne lifestyle on a lemonade income, don't panic and make sweeping changes. Instead, follow the advice in this programme to get all aspects of your finances in shape. This will give you long-lasting control over your money.

Remember that if you use any kind of credit, then this borrowed money may have soaked up some of your excess spending. The aim is to stop borrowing, pay off what you owe and then start saving. In the meantime, looking at your spending in detail will mean that you can spot overspending to avoid sliding further into debt. There are also many ways for you to reduce the cost of your debts and pay them off faster, as you'll discover in the coming days and weeks.

'Money never made a man happy yet, nor will it. There is nothing in its nature to produce happiness. The more a man has, the more he wants. Instead of filling a vacuum, it makes one.' Benjamin Franklin, US President

Because your budget breaks down your expenditure into 'essential', 'everyday' and 'occasional' categories, it's now much easier to spot where you can afford to cut back if you need to and where the problems are cropping up. This will also help you to plan your finances and avoid any nasty surprises such as big bills for annual costs like your car insurance.

No one's suggesting you stop having fun or enjoying simple pleasures. It's just that being aware of small amounts can give you the option of trading them in for something bigger, such as a holiday.

Using the bank statements you organised in Step 3 will help you sort out any direct debits or standing orders attached to your bank account. It's good financial practice to keep these under review, but it may also throw up things you had forgotten you were paying for.

Did you know?

Research from the bank Cahoot reveals that more than 80 per cent of us carry on paying for two or more months for a gym membership we don't use anymore. Magazine subscriptions and mobile phone contracts are other items that go unnoticed. If you're not sure what you're paying for, ask your bank for a list of your direct debits and standing orders and make sure you review them regularly.

Finally, preparing your budget is not a one-off. You should review it a couple of times a year and whenever your circumstances change. Managing your bank account online as explained in Step 4 will also help you keep tabs on your cash.

Activity

Cut back and save

- Go through the lists of everyday spending and occasional costs and ask yourself: 'Is this absolutely necessary?' This book will also explain ways to save money on essential costs, including your mortgage and bills.

- Consider how several small, short-term purchases can be sacrificed for more substantial or longer-term goals.

- Tick the boxes below if you regularly buy any of the items listed. Then see how much you can save.

Item	Average cost	Monthly cost	How much you could save per year	Tick box
CD	£9.99 a week	£40.00	£480.00	
Coffee	£1.50 each working day	£30.00	£330.00	
Lip gloss	£8.99 a month	£8.99	£108.00	
Shoes	£80 every month	£80.00	£960.00	
Gym	£40 a month	£40.00	£480.00	
Total potential saving				

BUDGET CLEANSE

Your notes

CHAPTER 3

CUT OUT TOXIC SPENDING

Now that you've a clearer idea of how much you're spending and where the money's going, it will be easier to identify why you're spending and how you can cut back. Ask yourself the following questions to help:

◆ Are you buying lunch from a sandwich bar every day because you can never seem to organise packed lunches?
◆ Do you shop for clothes and accessories when you're bored?
◆ Are you buying to distract yourself from a less exciting task or goal?
◆ Do you spend more because time always seems short and you need the quickest option, regardless of cost?
◆ Does your cash trickle away in a dozen different directions leaving you broke before the end of the month?

CASE STUDY

Mimi was bored and miserable at work but rather than channeling her frustration into looking for a new job, she resented her time in the office and started to spend her lunch hours comfort-buying. Usually it would be a book or DVD but once the habit started, it was hard to contemplate coming back to the office without a new item to cheer herself up.

Activity

Spot spending triggers

Using your money diary, together with your budget and your bank and credit card statements, see if you can find any patterns:

- If you tend to go crazy and blow lots of cash either on or just after pay day then it may be that you see your newly replenished bank balance as a bottomless pit. Banking online will help you keep a closer eye on your balance as it shrinks throughout the month.

- If you want to avoid temptation then set up an automatic monthly transfer of half your disposable income so that it disappears to a separate savings account before you can get your mitts on it.

- Transferring funds back to your current account when and if you need them can be done instantly online, but you should aim to set a target for the amount of disposable income you spend each month and spend only within that amount.

'If you want to know what God thinks of money, just look at the people he gave it to.' Dorothy Parker, author

CUT OUT TOXIC SPENDING

Ever felt so bored and fed up with the idea of sorting out your money that you just gave up and spent more? Many people binge-spend when they feel depressed about their finances. They take the view that they're already in debt so may as well max their credit card or blow their overdraft completely to cheer themselves up.

When credit kicks in

You should by now have a clear picture of where and why your disposable income runs out, as well as when – and by how much – you start depending on credit each month. If you're managing to pay off little more than the minimum amount on your credit card balance, then you're unlikely to ever clear the debt on it because constant spending and mounting interest eat into your repayments.

Are you paying off enough?

Paying off part of your credit card balance only to run it up to the limit again in the same month means you're 'robbing Peter to pay Paul'. In other words, you're spending money you can't really afford and being charged interest on it, month in and month out, without ever making any progress in getting your finances straight. It's time to break the cycle.

Activity

Break spending and debt cycles

If you view any spare credit as part of your available funds then it's time to rethink your spending. Chapter 4 on debt (Steps 16 to 22) will help you get your credit under control. In the meantime, look for opportunities to avoid using your flexible friend. These might include:

- Leave your credit card at home when you go shopping or on days when you might be tempted to splurge, such as immediately after you've paid part or all of your credit card bill.

- If you buy a round at the bar and choose to pay by credit card then don't set up a tab. This will encourage you to run up a bigger bill, particularly as the evening goes on and drinking may make you feel more generous.

- When you go to the supermarket, take enough cash to pay for what you *need* to buy and leave your cards at home so that you're not tempted to fill up your trolley 'because it's all going on the card, so it doesn't matter'.

CUT OUT TOXIC SPENDING

Activity

Helping you to spend less

A lot of things we buy aren't essential. Sometimes they're not even necessary but purely lazy or indulgent. We all do it, often because it's quicker or easier. But there are several key questions you can ask yourself to help you think twice before you spend:

- **'If I had to draw out the cash to buy this, would I be so keen to have it?'**

  Parting with cash is much harder than entering your PIN into a credit card machine. Don't let credit lull you into a false sense of riches.

- **'Does this suit me or am I buying it for the designer brand or because it's in the sale?'**

  Finding a bargain is exciting, but only if it's something you really want or need.

- **'If I saw this item with a less attractive brand on the label, would it still appeal?'**

  Whether it's an electrical gadget or a new dress, don't be seduced into paying more for the name on an item that might not otherwise be your cup of tea.

- **'Is there an own-brand version of this available for less?'**

  This applies everywhere from the supermarket to a boutique. Own brands are usually every bit as good as their more expensive counterparts. If in doubt, ask an assistant for advice on a specific item.

- **'Once I pay the interest on my credit card, how much will this really cost me?'**

  If you don't completely clear your credit card balance every month then you can add up to 20 per cent onto the cost of your item.

- **'This may be on special offer, but is it even worth the reduced amount?'**

  When is a bargain not a bargain? When you're really only buying it because you think you're getting it for less.

- **'Even though this is buy-one, get-one-free, will I really use it?'**

  It's hard to resist a give-away but if you don't use hair mousse then you're not likely to start.

- **'If I buy this, will it mean I can't afford other things?'**

  It's one thing to splurge on something you see, but will spending that money reduce your options on other purchases or activities later in the month?

'Money can't buy everything – that's what credit cards are for.'
Ruby Wax, comedian

CUT OUT TOXIC SPENDING

You wouldn't be human if you cut shopping out of your life altogether. But your chances of overspending and breaking your budget can be greatly reduced by a little bit of forward thinking and planning before you head off to the shops.

A key danger zone

The supermarket provides a classic opportunity to spend more than you planned. It may sound cynical, but these stores are designed to seduce you with items you didn't plan to buy and make you feel good about doing it.

The way to beat the system is to draw up a shopping list before you go. Many people find this is a must have, if only to help them remember everything from one week to the next. But your list can help you stick to buying just what you need.

Be single-minded and never go food shopping when you're hungry. Planning the food and meals you need for the week could also save you shopping time.

 TOP TIP

◆ If the supermarket layout is familiar to you, then you can head straight to the aisles for the items you need to buy and avoid the temptation of extras.

Activity

Stick to lists and avoid temptation

- If shopping is your weak spot – and you should know this by now from your money diary – then lists could be the key to cutting back.

- Make a note of what you need, from birthday cards to dental floss, from picture hooks to hoop earrings. This will help you avoid overspending. Of course, writing things you don't need and can't afford in a list doesn't mean you should buy them.

- Try not to head to shopping centres for browsing. Instead, make sure any shopping trip fits in with your budget and has a clear agenda.

- Put less time on your parking ticket if you want to limit your risk of a splurge.

'I was once so poor I didn't know where my next husband was coming from.' Mae West, actress

CUT OUT TOXIC SPENDING

If you've been juggling poor cash flow and growing debt for a while, then you've probably already found that you've missed out on things you simply can't afford. Whether you have to forego the latest gadget, a holiday with friends or something truly life-changing such as the deposit for a flat, it's a frustrating feeling.

Think big

Your grandparents may have told you that 'if you look after the pennies, the pounds will take care of themselves'. While financial happiness may not seem that simple, it certainly helps to be aware of a trickle of spending that can drain your bank account.

TOP TIP

◆ When you spend money, think carefully, 'Do I really want this more than a holiday/flat/car?' Your targets don't have to be huge but planning your finances will help you avoid wondering where all your money has gone at the end of every month.

Activity

Consider how to make your dreams come true

- Think about the financial and lifestyle goals you want to achieve in the coming months or even years.

- Your budget will show you just how close you are to achieving the first of them.

- You should also be able to work out how much you need to save and how long it might take you to reach your first goal.

- Once you have a target figure, think about smaller, less expensive things that eat up your cash but that you could do without in order to achieve your bigger goal.

- Start with a realistic target and use your budget to help you set a date by which you can afford the first goal.

Getting to your first goal will inspire you to go further. And your targets may not all be about buying things for yourself – you may want to buy something extra special for the birthday of a friend or family member. Aims such as paying off a certain amount of debt or saving enough to keep you debt-free next Christmas may feature in your list.

CUT OUT TOXIC SPENDING

Your notes

CHAPTER 4

DEBT AEROBICS

It's easy to get so used to borrowing money through overdrafts, loans and credit cards that we don't see this as debt but as an extension of our income. When your credit card issuer increases the limit on your card, it's not out of the goodness of their heart. It's designed to encourage you to borrow more and pay back an even greater amount of interest! If you think you may be in debt but are not sure, then take the following test.

Quick quiz

Debt test

Answer 'yes' or 'no' to the following questions:

Do you:

- have more than two credit cards with constantly rising balances?

- pay just the monthly minimum for each credit card?

- have long standing store card debt?

- borrow from one source to pay off another debt?

- have trouble paying for essentials – mortgage, bills, food?

- have loans taken out to repay other debts, which then accumulates more borrowing?

- find that you run out of money long before pay day every month?

- regularly miss loan repayments?

- regularly pay for basics such as grocery shopping with credit cards?

- face legal action by lenders?

- dread the arrival of the post and put off opening bills?

- argue with a partner over debts?

If you answered 'yes' to three or more of these questions then it's time to confront your debts and get your finances back on track.

Activity

Organise your debt

- Make a list of all the ways you borrow money, including credit cards, store cards, loans, overdrafts, benefits overpayments, hire purchase agreements for non-essential items such as a television, catalogue arrears and anything you've borrowed from family or friends.

- Write down exactly how much you owe to each lender and check your statements and any loan agreements for the interest rate on each.

- Organising the information like this will make tackling the debts much easier.

'My last credit card bill was so big, before I opened it I actually heard a drum roll.'
Rita Rudner, comedian

IOU

Visa £800 @ 8% interest

Bloggs store card £230 @ 27% interest

Mum and Dad £300 @ 0% interest

Now you have a clear view of your credit and loan debts, you also need to consider other bills and make sure the most important ones get paid first. Money you owe should be divided into 'priority' and 'non-priority' debts.

Activity

Get your debts in order

Start by listing any priority debts. These include your mortgage or rent, any loans secured on your home, council tax, child support, hire purchase plans and utilities bills. These are debts owed to creditors that can take the strongest legal actions against you if you don't pay. It's not the size of the debt that makes it a priority, but what the creditors can do to recover their money. For example:

- If you have mortgage or rent arrears, the lender or landlord can repossess your home or evict you.

- Unpaid utilities bills mean your electricity, gas or telephone can be disconnected and you'll then face reconnection charges.

- With unpaid maintenance, child support, council tax or fines a court can use bailiffs to repossess your goods. If, after this, you still have arrears unpaid, you can be sent to prison.

- Owing unpaid income tax or VAT means you can be made bankrupt or imprisoned for non-payment.

- Hire purchase agreements on essential items, for instance where you buy a vehicle for work, are also priority debts.

DEBT AEROBICS

TOP TIP

- Don't dodge the letters or phone calls but be honest about the amount you can repay and discuss what new level of interest the creditors plan to impose. Sensible communication is the first step to resolving the problem.

Understanding non-priority debt

Examples of non-priority debts are the ones you listed in Step 16. You can't be imprisoned for not paying non-priority debts and you're unlikely to lose your home. However, if you make no offers to pay, without explaining why, the creditors will take you to court. They may sell on the unpaid debt you owe them to a licensed debt collection agency, which will then chase you for the money.

FACT: If you have any priority debts, you must make sure you can maintain them before you consider how much you have left to repay your non-priority debts.

Picture the scene ... you've taken your credit card right up to the limit and won't be making another payment on it for two weeks. The trouble is, you'd love to buy that new pair of shoes, DVD player or earrings. Instead of thinking, 'I can't afford it,' the temptation is to think, 'How can I find a way to buy it?' It may be on offer but that doesn't make it right for you ...

It's very easy to borrow money – whether it's through plastic cards, loans, overdrafts or credit arrangements. Many people argue that the banks wouldn't offer them credit if it wasn't a good idea. But banks and other financial companies want to make money. If you can't pay off your credit card bill in full and owe them interest every month, then you'll be their best friend.

 TOP TIP

- ◆ It's no coincidence that many credit card issuers and banks will send you loan offers after you have built up a large balance which you are struggling to pay off. Resist temptation.

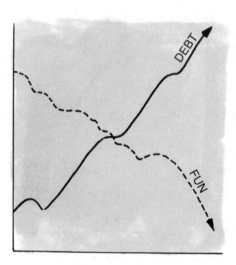

Activity

Remember to keep saying no

- It's crucial to remember that your credit card limit is not your money. You're borrowing the money and will have to pay it back, probably with interest. So when letters arrive in the post offering you loans or new credit cards, these are not opportunities to buy things you can't afford. They're the route to more debt.

- However much you feel you can't get the things you want in life without stretching your debt just a little bit further, this will make you miserable in the long run. Taking on more debt is not a way out. It will push your chances of ever getting straight even further away. When new offers of credit arrive in the post, don't even open them, but shred them or tear them into small pieces (this also avoids the risk of identity theft, as covered later in Step 93).

TOP TIP

- If your credit card issuer increases your credit limit on an existing card, you'll need to exercise great willpower and call them to decline the rise. The same applies to your bank, which may bump up your overdraft. Just say, 'no thank you'.

DEBT AEROBICS

As well as cutting back on spending and avoiding extra debt, aim to make existing debts as cheap as possible while you pay them off. In other words, look for ways to reduce the amount of interest you're paying on the money you owe.

Roll several debts into one

Many people are tempted to take out one debt to pay off another – a process called 'debt consolidation'. If you're trying to pay off debts with several different lenders and find yourself juggling cash every month, then rolling all your debts into one could make life easier. Not only does it mean you have one payment to make each month instead of several, but the new debt will have one rate of interest, ideally lowering the amount you pay overall.

A popular way of doing this is through a personal loan. These lump sums can be borrowed from banks, building societies and loan companies. They're usually arranged for a fixed period and interest rate, with monthly repayments made by direct debit. They can make your debt cheaper and easier to manage, but the key is always to only borrow what you can afford or you run the risk of making your debts worse.

Activity

Debt homework

● Start by looking for other credit cards that offer you the chance to transfer your balance from an existing card and pay 0 per cent – zero-interest – while you pay it off. Some cards offer the 0 per cent period for a fixed time, such as six months, but you may find a card that offers longer or a very reduced amount of interest until the balance is completely paid off.

● You should also shop around carefully for a loan as the interest rates on offer vary enormously. Think carefully before you sign up for any loan payment protection. This is covered in more detail in Step 47. Most importantly, resist rolling several unsecured loans into a loan secured on your home.

FACT: Whether you switch credit cards or take out a loan, it's crucial that you cut up the cards you've paid off to resist the urge to use them again and so take on more debt. *Skint to Mint* will also explain later in the programme how to save by switching your mortgage or overdraft.

Just as it's easy to borrow money and get credit, there are firms that specialise in trying to lend you more money to pay off existing debts. Beware! Most debt-management companies are only interested in customers who own their own home so that the property can be used as surety against the debts. This means that 'unsecured' credit card or loan debts suddenly become 'secured' against your home. Put simply, if you fail to make the repayments, you could lose your home. It's that serious. You may also find that you have to pay substantial fees and that your debt repayments only appear cheaper because you're now repaying over ten years instead of two.

A healthier alternative

By following the steps in this book, you've already begun your own debt management. This involves looking in detail at your budget, assessing how much you owe and then working out where you can cut back and what money you have available to pay off your debts in a steady, affordable way.

Activity

DIY debt management

- Set aside an affordable amount of cash each month to start reducing your debts.

- Use your budget to help you work out how much you can spare.

- It may be most effective to pay regular amounts by direct debit just after you get paid, so that you don't miss the money and will have a clear idea of what cash is left each month after your payments have been made.

DEBT AEROBICS

Hang in there!

As you begin to reduce your debt, you may find it hard to adjust to the changes in your lifestyle. Apart from anything else, you'll have a regular amount of money disappearing from your account each month and no shopping to show for it. Where you were once spending without thinking, you may now be more restricted in how far your cash will stretch. If you have a blip and blow some cash, then look at it as a minor setback and recalculate your budget for that month. But don't give up.

TOP TIP

◆ If you still think you need professional debt consolidation and management, you can get a free service from Payplan, an independent company that's funded by the credit industry. Details are available in Step 21.

'A billion here, a billion there, and pretty soon you're talking about real money.' US Senator Everett Dirksen

DEBT AEROBICS

Being in debt can be a lonely and frightening experience. Hoping your money problems will go away is the worst thing you can do. If you fail to pay your rent or mortgage then you're at risk of losing the roof over your head. Ignoring bills and credit card debts will mean you end up owing more money and risk damaging your long-term credit prospects with late or missed payments.

Activity

Be honest about your debts and seek help

The first step to financial recovery is admitting that you're in trouble. The next is seeking help. Ask yourself:

- Do you owe more than you thought?

- Are you worried about how you will pay off your debts?

- Are you struggling to make minimum payments?

- Is interest on what you owe mounting up?

If you answer 'yes' to even one of these questions then talking to an expert could provide the help you need.

There are several national organisations that provide counselling, advice or just a friendly ear if you have concerns about money.

The Citizens' Advice Bureaux

Helps resolve legal, money and other problems by providing free information and advice from over 3,200 locations.
Check your phone directory for your local office.

The Consumer Credit Counselling Service (CCCS)

A registered charity that assists people who are in financial difficulty by providing free, independent, impartial and realistic advice. The CCCS can assess your situation and ask creditors to freeze interest, stop penalties, accept a longer repayment period and sometimes a reduced sum.
Call 0800 138 1111 or go online at: www.cccs.co.uk

National Debtline

A telephone helpline for people with debt problems in England, Wales and Scotland. The service is free, confidential and independent. Specialist advice given over the telephone is backed up with free self-help materials and guides. It may also be able to set up a free debt-management plan for you.
Call 0808 808 4000 or go online at: www.nationaldebtline.co.uk

Payplan

One of the UK's leading debt-management companies – and its services are free. It can help you to set up and keep to a manageable repayment plan for your debts and undertake regular reviews of your circumstances to ensure that your Payplan arrangement is still working. The arrangement then continues until all of your debts are cleared.
Call 0800 085 4298 or go online at: www.payplan.com

The Samaritans

Provide confidential emotional support, 24 hours a day for people who are experiencing feelings of distress or despair, including those that may lead to suicide. They're there for you if you're worried about something, feel upset or confused, or you just want to talk to someone.
Call 08457 90 90 90.

DEBT AEROBICS

The broken heart or ideas of revenge you may experience at the end of a relationship are bad enough. The last thing you want to add to this is a pile of bills and debts when you and your partner split up.

Activity
Limit any damage

If you think you may be about to break up with your partner, there are steps you can take to limit any financial damage:

- Generally speaking, you're not liable for your partner's – or anyone else's debts – unless you signed an agreement or acted as guarantor.

- Make a list of any joint finances. If you've taken out a mortgage, credit agreement, a loan, or have a bank account in joint names, then you're both liable – jointly and individually – for the full amount of any debt. This is known as 'joint and several liability' and also applies to rent arrears on joint tenancies, arrears on joint mortgages, council tax payments and water charges on properties that have been jointly occupied.

- If you take out a joint mortgage then you'll be jointly and individually liable for the debt. Talk to your lender straight away if you think there'll be a change in financial circumstances. It's crucial to keep in touch with your lender so that they'll view your circumstances sympathetically if you need their help.

Activity

If the going gets tough ...

- If your partner is refusing to pay their share of the monthly mortgage payments and you can meet them on your own for a short time, make sure you keep evidence to prove what you've contributed.

- If you can't meet the payments, you should have urgent talks with your lender. They may be able to reduce your payments or provide a payment holiday for a couple of months to ease the transition.

- If arrears have built up but you can start making payments, the lender may agree to spread the outstanding debt across the whole of your loan.

- Another alternative may be to alter your mortgage, by changing the type of repayment option or extending the length of the term, although these options will depend on your age and financial circumstances.

Your notes

....

....

....

....

....

....

....

....

....

....

....

....

....

....

....

CHAPTER 5

CASH TONE UP

One of the most important ways to stay financially healthy is by keeping your cash under control. After all, without it, you enter the bleak world of more debt and less fun. Keeping an eye on your bank balance, your disposable income and forthcoming bills will all help you assess and understand the 'big picture' of your money, instead of hiding from it.

Activity

Look closely at your cash

- Look for patterns in your bank accounts of cash withdrawals. Do you take what you need whenever you need it or do you draw out a limited amount each week? Now that you have a clear idea of your monthly disposable income, it should be easier to work out a weekly limit for cash withdrawals so that you curb any overspending.

- Another reason for avoiding lots of small, irregular cash withdrawals is that they make it harder to keep track of what's left in your account.

- Sticking to your limit and monitoring your account online will help you keep your finances steady throughout each month. There's nothing worse than running out of cash a week before pay day. This will usually mean you have to rely on credit so plan ahead to avoid the miserable run-up to getting paid again.

CASH TONE UP

FACT:
- If you find a weekly limit is not working for you then start with a daily amount and build up to handling larger amounts of cash over a slightly longer period.
- If you don't spend as much as you expect from your weekly limit, aim to hold onto the cash and make it last instead of letting it burn a hole in your pocket.
- Equally, if you overspend one week, then cut back a little the next.
- If you have disposable income left over at the end of the month, try to put it into your savings rather than spend it.

'Money is a good servant but a poor master.' Anonymous

Your current account is the heart of your finances, pumping cash to all the right places when you need it. It should be fit and flexible if it's to work hard for you.

Many of us stick with the same account we've had since we were children or the one we opened when we started our first job. Years ago, there were a handful of banks that all offered the same sort of services and rates. Now we're spoilt for choice and should shop around for the best home for our hard-earned money.

TOP TIP

♦ You may have been with the same bank for 15 years but that is unlikely to make any difference at all if you need any favours or special deals.

Few rewards

It would be a different story if your bank rewarded your loyalty and encouraged you not to move your account. But very few people get so much as a raised eyebrow from their bank manager if they take their custom elsewhere. We like to think we're good at shopping around for a good deal but more than two-thirds of us put up with a lousy deal, including non-existent interest and expensive overdrafts, from our bank.

Activity

Shop around

Make sure you compare as many different accounts as possible to find for the best for you.

- The latest trend is for banks to make a fixed monthly charge in return for extra privileges. Weigh up any extras along with the rates of interest paid and charges for overdrafts.

- Some banks operate purely online and by telephone so that the money they save by not running branches can be passed on to customers. Make sure the basic features work for you – that you can get your money in and out as easily as possible.

- Don't be distracted by freebies such as car breakdown cover or travel insurance. They may come with a bank account that doesn't deliver or overcharges.

- Ask a bank what procedures it has in place to help you switch your account across. This will give you a good feel for its customer service standards before you join it.

'A bank is a place where they lend you an umbrella in fair weather and ask for it back when it begins to rain.'
Robert Frost, poet

CASH TONE UP

If you decide you want to switch your current account then start by making a list of the things you're not happy with. This should help you identify a bank that can give you what you want.

Activity

Make the move

1 Shop around

Asking friends and relatives is helpful to a point but remember that everyone's finances and experiences are very different.

2 Open up

Once you've found your new bank, open an account. Make sure you tell them that you'll be switching from another bank so that they can help you make the move. Don't forget to request the transfer of any loans, overdrafts or other debts in your application. Wait until the new account is up and running before you do anything else.

3 Sign a switching mandate

Once your application has been accepted you'll be asked to sign a mandate enabling the new bank to act on your behalf during the switch. This allows it to get details of your direct debits and standing orders from your old bank and the companies you pay in this way. As it receives confirmation that each payment has been switched, the new bank will cancel the obsolete payments at your old bank.

4 Redirect your salary

Most importantly, write to your employer with your new bank account details so that your salary can be paid in. It may be best to do this just after your monthly salary has been paid, to allow time for the change to be made.

5 Close your old account

Once you're happy that your new account is up and running smoothly you can close down your old account by notifying your old bank in writing. Bear in mind this may take several weeks. You may have to keep the account open if you have debts that haven't been transferred to your new account. If your old bank takes an interest in why you're leaving, make sure you have your say. This is the only way banks will understand where they're going wrong.

TOP TIP

♦ Make sure that you set the dates for the freshly-moved standing orders and direct debits so that the bills are paid after your salary enters the account or at another convenient time.

CASH TONE UP

Back in the 1980s, shoulder pads were not the only things in fashion. If you wanted to buy something without using cash or a credit card then you wrote out a cheque. But as the costs of processing cheques rose, a fully electronic payment system was created that would reduce fraud and be more convenient for customers. This was the birth of Switch – one of the world's first domestic debit cards. This has now been replaced by Maestro – a debit card you can use at home and abroad.

The beauty of debit cards is that you can avoid carrying lots of cash or currency, or a cheque book, with you and you know that everything you spend comes directly from your current account so it's not building up debt in the way a credit card does.

FACT: Keeping your card safe and using the PIN (Personal Identification Number) with care will help protect your money and financial information from thieves and fraudsters.

Treat your debit card as carefully as you would the contents of your bank account because if it's lost, stolen or mis-used then the money will come out of your current account and it could take some time to resolve the problem and refund any stolen money.

For the same reasons, you should also keep your receipts from debit card transactions, which may carry your full card number and other information. Make sure you shred them when you've finished with them.

Activity

Become debit-friendly

- If you don't already have a debit card or if you have one with limited use, such as Solo, then try talking to your bank.

- If you're struggling to keep your current account in credit then your bank may want to see an improvement in your money management before they give you Maestro card.

TOP TIP

- If you find that you use a debit card a fair amount, then online banking will help you keep track of your spending. It's worth noting that some transactions take several days to come through your account so check carefully to ensure you're spending within your means.

The idea of getting through life for even a day without your credit cards may fill you with dread, but imagine trying it for a week. Today's activity involves just that.

This exercise is designed to re-acquaint you with money, remind you of the value of things you buy and make you think twice about your spending habits. It's so much easier to hand over a plastic card when you buy something, particularly if you know you can't really afford it.

This is particularly relevant with high-street spending where you can kid yourself that £50 here or there may not make a huge difference. In reality, if you had to hand over five £10 notes you might feel very differently about what you've bought. Many of us rely on plastic and it's easier to keep stretching our finances when we don't have to think beyond entering our four-digit PIN number.

 TOP TIP

♦   If this cash-only challenge works well for you, then you can try it again in future for a day or longer if you feel the need to get a firmer grip on your finances or give your credit cards a break.

Activity

Go credit cold-turkey

Using your budget to work out your disposable income, calculate how much cash you'll need to withdraw for each day or, better still, a whole week. Leave your credit cards at home – all of them – and brave the real world! If you normally use a debit card, avoid paying with it and stick to cash.

Aim to stick with cash for a week but take it one day at a time and see how long you can last. At the end of your cash challenge, consider:

- How many times did you decide not to buy something because spending cash rather than using plastic made the item seem less appealing?

- If you decided against spending money at certain times, did this make you feel better about your finances, as if you were taking a step towards getting back on track?

- Did you have less fun and less freedom using cash or did it feel more liberating and give you a sense of control?

You may not know it but you could be sitting on a small, forgotten fortune. There is an estimated £15 billion languishing in the form of unclaimed shares, pensions, bank accounts, insurance policies and premium bonds. This amounts to more than £1,000 for every household in the country. It's estimated that about one in four people may be owed some money. Some of it could be yours!

It's out there somewhere

◆ Around £3 billion is languishing in National Savings post-office accounts, certificates and premium bonds.
◆ Just as much in shares and dividends is waiting to be claimed, mostly from windfall shares following privatisation or building-society demutualisation.
◆ Estimates of the amount lying unclaimed in occupational pension schemes range between £500m and a staggering £77 billion according to Opra, the regulator for occupational pension schemes. Tracing a pension through Opra's registry is free and approximately one-third of the inquiries made in 2005 resulted in successful claims.

Beware of bounty hunters

Of course, with all this money sloshing around, it's no surprise that less scrupulous characters are trying to cash in. Beware of bounty hunters who claim to find your fortune in return for a large fee or percentage. It's much easier and much cheaper to do it yourself. If you know the name of the company then contact them directly with as many details as possible.

Alternatively try the Unclaimed Assets Register (go to: www.uar.co.uk), managed by data giant Experian. By passing them a few personal details, including past and present addresses, they can search for any lost fortunes on their database. You don't even have to remember the name of the financial company involved, although as much information as possible will help.

Remember that simply having a policy doesn't guarantee that money is due – it may already have been paid out or have lapsed if premiums were not kept up to date. A general search costs £18 with 10 per cent of that fee going to charity.

Activity

Look for forgotten treasure

- Think about any old savings accounts or policies that you may have forgotten you have.

- Dig out any old financial documents that you can follow up that will help you claim any money you find.

Although not as fashionable as they were in the last century, almost half of all couples open joint accounts. On the plus side, they're seen as a statement of commitment and trust, particularly if one partner earns more than the other. They're also a practical approach to shared expenses such as bills and mortgage payments.

Go for a 'three-way'

A joint account can also create problems if you don't stop to consider the approach you each have to spending. Imagine the cashpoint rejecting your card because your other half has frittered away your hard-earned cash on new golf clubs or designer handbags! A compromise is to each have a personal account in addition to your joint account.

This 'three-pot system' means that you can each enjoy some financial freedom while your mortgage or rent and any joint bills are covered by your joint account. For similar reasons, separate savings accounts give you each more control and, in a modern age of internet banking, transfers can be made between accounts in a few seconds, when needed.

CASE STUDY

When Sacha moved into the house that Dan already owned they needed to make joint financial arrangements for the mortgage and bills, and also took legal advice to protect the money Dan had already invested in the property. They trusted each other completely and had open discussions about money so there was no tension or awkwardness. Talking about money will always help avoid problems.

CASH TONE UP

Activity

Consider the pros and cons of joint finances

- If you and a partner are planning to combine your finances, then discuss the details and be aware of the risks before you go ahead.

- As well as enjoying shared cash, you also share individual and joint responsibility for any debt that was taken out between you. So think carefully about overdraft limits. If one of you goes overdrawn then you're both liable, jointly and individually, which means the bank can chase you for money that your partner spent.

- You may want the flexibility of limitless, single-signature withdrawals from a joint account, but it could then be drained by either one of you. Most banks provide the option of a limit on the size of withdrawals beyond your standing-order payments or insist on both signatures for additional withdrawals from the account.

- Understanding all the options will give you financial confidence.

Since 1996, the gas and electricity markets have opened up, helping to bring energy prices down as competing firms undercut each other. But if you're one of the 26 million domestic electricity customers or the 20 million gas customers, then you could cut your bills by switching one or both providers.

What you could save

Energy regulator Ofgem says the biggest gain is for customers who have never switched. It believes they could save around £100 on their annual home energy bill and perhaps more if they change the way they pay. The reason is that if you've never moved supplier then you're probably still getting your energy from what was once a monopoly supplier and being charged their highest tariff.

What else you need to know

Moving to a new supplier isn't risky. Most suppliers are large, trusted companies and all of them are regulated to ensure standards of service. Some suppliers offer combined plans to customers who choose to have both their gas and electricity supplied by a single company. These plans are often referred to as 'dual fuel' deals, and typically include incentives and reduced prices. If you're interested in green energy tariffs then uSwitch can show an alphabetical list.

Activity

Shop around, switch and save

- Switching energy companies is easy to do. Start by making use of the free, impartial comparison websites that are accredited by Energywatch, such as SwitchwithWhich, uSwitch and MoneyExpert – it will only take a few minutes of your time.

- If you decide to make the switch after your energy comparison, you'll need to fill in some personal details, which will be passed straight on to your new supplier.

- The switching process usually takes between four to six weeks.

TOP TIP

Consumer campaigners Which? suggest these ways to save money on your utility bills:
- Pay by direct debit – all companies should give you a discount for doing this.
- Using the same supplier for gas and electricity may also save you cash – check out dual fuel tariffs.
- Be more energy efficient – contact the Energy Savings Trust 020 7222 0101 or call your energy supplier and ask them for advice on how to be more energy efficient.

'Money won't create success, the freedom to make it will.'
Nelson Mandela, civil rights leader

CASH TONE UP

Now you're getting into the hang of comparing services and switching to save money, let's look at your home phone. There are now almost 200 licensed phone companies in the UK, each offering different tariffs and packages according to the types of phone calls they provide, such as local, national and international calls. Some of these phone companies are household names such as BT, while others are less well known. What this means for you is a world of competitive offers and savings to be made on your bills.

TOP TIP

♦ You may be happy with your current phone company but until you compare prices and services, you won't know whether a better deal is available elsewhere.

FACT: One area where it's tough to find cheaper rates is on calls from landlines to mobile phones. These can be quite high because landline suppliers are constrained by the rates charged by mobile network providers to call their networks.

What you could save

Switching to a cheaper deal could save you as much as £150 a year. uSwitch also rates the companies using customer feedback on areas such as customer service, online usability and how long they take to respond to emails, so you can get better value for money all round.

Activity

Shop around, switch and save

- Think about how and when you use your phone most. If you regularly make international calls, then some providers specialise in cheaper overseas tariffs. Others may offer cheaper rates if you usually make most of your calls at evenings or weekends.

- It's now easier than ever to shop around using a home-telephone comparison service such as the free and impartial calculators offered by www.uSwitch.com. You may find other similar, services but, at the time of writing, uSwitch is the only home-telephone calculator that is approved by the regulator OFCOM. As a result, the site has to comply with a strict code of practice that includes holding accurate and up-to-date pricing.

- uSwitch will ask you questions about your telephone usage and search hundreds of tariffs to provide a list of options, based on your requirements, which could save you money compared with your existing provider. Once you've chosen a new telephone company, they can even arrange the switch for you.

CASH TONE UP

There's never been more choice of mobile phone providers and packages so shopping around could save you money every month.

What you could save

Pre-pay tariffs, where you buy the phone and top up the credit, are ideal if you want a mobile only for emergencies or to receive calls. They're also handy for people who want to manage their call costs.

As a rule of thumb, consumer campaigner Which? recommends that if your bill is more than £15 a month and you use your phone for more than three minutes a day, you might save money with a contract. In fact, its research shows that almost ten million pre-pay users would be better off on a contract.

Those already on a contract could save almost £100 a year by moving when they renew. But three-quarters of mobile users have never considered switching to a better deal.

What else you need to know

All contract tariffs include line rental, a fixed monthly fee that can range from £5 to over £50. Contract charges usually cover the costs of a certain number of 'free' minutes or texts, but it's essential to make sure that you'll really use what you're paying for, otherwise you could be better off on a different tariff.

TOP TIP

Steven Day of Virgin Mobile advises:

◆ Don't be seduced by hardware – look beyond a trendy phone to the running costs.

◆ Make sure voicemail is free to use. An average of one in ten calls go through to voicemail, but this figure is higher for younger users.

◆ Avoid air-time, top-ups or text packages that run out at the end of each month if they're not used.

Activity

Shop around, switch and save

● To keep saving, review how much you use your phone: when you make calls, how often you text and whether you plan to take your phone abroad. Then pick the provider that offers the best deal on everything you need plus some extras.

● If you find the amount of choice confusing, use an independent comparison service such as Which?'s free SwitchwithWhich website. This compares more than 300 tariffs from leading providers and is updated every month when providers announce their latest tariffs. It's also quick and easy to use. You can also try other independent comparison services such as OneCompare.

CASH TONE UP

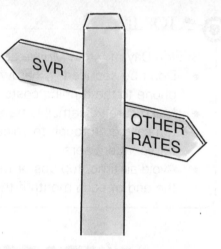

Homeowners are three times more likely to shop around for their car insurance than think about how to switch to a better deal on their biggest financial commitment – their mortgage – according to the Department of Trade and Industry. More than a quarter of us are paying our lender's standard variable rate (SVR) on our mortgage. This type of rate will go up or down as the lender adjusts it to economic and market conditions. It's usually the most uncompetitive rate to be on and its fluctuations won't suit those who want to pay a set amount every month.

 **TOP TIP**

♦ With more than 4,000 different mortgages available, it makes sense to shop around and learn as much as possible so that you can choose the best possible deal for you.

Why you need to shop around

Apparently, the average UK borrower would only remortgage if they could save at least £93 a month according to research from high-street bank Bradford & Bingley. This 'trigger point' reflects homeowners' desire to save money on their monthly repayments, but only if the price is right.

What you could save

Almost a third of borrowers are put off remortgaging because they think it takes a lot of time and hassle. A similar number think it would be expensive to switch deals. Some homeowners don't know where to start and others believe they can only remortgage if they're moving home.

These myths and misconceptions are costing us a fortune. Bradford & Bingley reveal that some 3.3 million mortgage holders could potentially save around £6 billion a year in mortgage payments if they switched from their current SVR rate onto a market-leading deal.

The following example highlights the potential savings you could make: a homeowner with a £100,000 mortgage on an average SVR could save around £150 a month (£1,800 a year) by remortgaging to a market-leading deal.

Activity

Review your home loan

- If you've got a mortgage, now's the time to check what rate of interest you're paying. Lots of homeowners get their loan and then forget about it for years.

- Are you paying your lender's standard variable rate? If you are, then you can almost certainly save money. If you're not then it's still worth shopping around as you could be paying less every month.

Activity

Shop around, switch and save

Today's the day to get to grips with your biggest financial commitment. If you think you could save money by switching then here's how to make the change:

1 Decide what you want to get out of your mortgage review

Do you want lower monthly payments, the security of a fixed rate, a capital sum for a holiday or home improvements, flexibility or debt consolidation?

2 Check your existing mortgage

What's your current mortgage rate? How much do you pay every month? Are you tied into any fixed-rate or discounted deal and for how long? Check you're not going to be subject to a penalty.

3 Get a redemption statement

Ask your current lender for a written redemption statement, which will show the exact outstanding balance of your loan, the remaining term and any fees or penalties you'll be charged for redeeming your mortgage.

4 Shop around among other lenders for a better deal

It's best to collect and compare information from at least five lenders, but you can get an independent broker to scour the market for you. When comparing the savings you'd make on different deals, look behind the headline rate and monthly payments on offer. Ask for details of the up-front costs and if the deal means paying for any compulsory insurances.

5 Decide if you want to stay with your existing company

Once you've gathered the information, you'll be in a strong position to go back to your existing lender. Lenders don't always make re-mortgaging easy for their own customers. Many refuse to offer the best deals to customers who want to re-mortgage rather than move house, saying the latter have more expenses. Only when customers threaten to take their business elsewhere do some relent and reveal their best 'under the counter' deals.

6 Gather together your paperwork

Depending upon whether you stay with your own lender or move lenders, you'll need proof of ID, residence and income. You'll also be asked for one year's mortgage statements, between one and three months' payslips, between one and three months' bank statements, a P60 certificate of pay and tax deducted, and sometimes an employer's reference. Being prepared means you can start saving as soon as possible.

Now that your budget has made everything clear and you're cutting your spending and debt while boosting your cash, it's time to think about savings. It's certainly true that spending is more fun than saving, but putting money aside makes sense for all sorts of reasons.

Today's activity deals with building up an emergency stash of cash.

Quick quiz

Emergency cash quiz

It's essential to have the security of knowing you can dip into some rainy-day savings if you're caught short by unforeseen circumstances. If you're not sure what sort of thing would push your finances to the limit unexpectedly, then ask yourself the following questions:

- If my car, washing machine or central heating broke down, could I afford to have it mended as soon as possible?

- If there was a computer error and my monthly salary did not get paid on time, would I have enough to live on without panicking?

- If my best friend suddenly decided to get married in Australia, would I be able to jump on a plane when I most wanted to?

If these examples make it clear that you would be stuck if you suddenly needed cash then it's time to start saving.

How much should you save?

Emergency savings don't have to be about a crisis. They're a fundamental part of your financial planning. The amount you save depends on your circumstances and lifestyle. For instance, if you rent rather than own your home, then a landlord would take care of many domestic pitfalls. Then again, if you're self-employed you'll need a buffer to cover short-term payment delays, a drop in demand for work or a period of illness.

As a rule of thumb, aim to save three months' living expenses.

Activity

Open your emergency savings account

- Choose your rainy-day savings account carefully.

- By its very nature an emergency fund should be something you can access instantly. For this reason it also makes sense to use an account that provides a cashcard so you can get to your money outside banking hours.

- Remember to keep the card safe but out of temptation's way.

- Avoid accounts that require notice, even though they may earn you more interest.

- Ideally, you'll also need a non-existent or high limit on the amount that can be withdrawn.

CASH TONE UP

Once you have money set aside for emergencies, it's time to think about your other short- to medium-term savings goals that are coming up in the next one to five years.

Dos and don'ts

◆ Do think about how long you can afford to tie your cash up for and whether you may need instant access.

◆ Don't take capital risks with this money. It may be tempting to try to make more cash through stockmarket investments, but these carry a risk and you may not get back the money you put in.

◆ Do shop around regularly – at least twice a year – for the best interest rates and be prepared to switch for a better return. The comparative tables provided by the money watchdog, the Financial Services Authority (FSA), provide free, independent information to help you decide. Find these online at: www.fsa.gov.uk/consumer/compare

Activity

Open a short- to medium-term savings account

When looking for a home for these savings, it makes sense to consider an account that pays a good rate of interest on your money. Beyond the comfort of instant access accounts, consider:

- No notice accounts tend to offer slightly better rates than instant access because the account is usually run via telephone and/or post and your money can take a couple of days to reach you by cheque or transfer.

- Internet-only accounts usually provide flexibility for web-surfing savers. They can offer competitive rates because their costs are low and many offer attractive introductory deals – but look at the rates beyond these before you open an account. If you'd like the security of telephone back up, find out whether this is offered and if you'll be charged for calls. Crucially, make sure you know how to get your money out.

- Notice accounts generally pay you higher interest on the basis that you give notice for any withdrawals. You'll have to wait between one and three months to get access to your money, although instant access is usually possible subject to an interest penalty of between 30 to 100 days on the money you withdraw. It therefore makes sense to only open a notice account if you can be sure of planning your withdrawals in advance.

- Mini or cash ISAs are covered in more detail in the next step but can be a very useful way of saving for income taxpayers.

CASH TONE UP

If you pay income tax then an ideal place for your savings could be in an Individual Savings Account – or ISA. These were introduced by the government in 1999 to replace PEPs and TESSAs. As a taxpayer, you normally have to pay tax on any interest you earn on the money you put into standard bank and building-society savings accounts. ISAs are a tax-free wrapper where you can put savings or investments. They represent one of the few tax-breaks available.

How much can you save in an ISA?

The current rules on ISAs mean that each tax year, from 6 April one year to 5 April the following year, if you're 18 or older, you can invest up to £7,000 in ISAs.

You can either take out:

◆ one 'maxi' ISA, in which you can invest up to £7,000 all in stocks and shares or split between the three components (stocks and shares, cash and insurance) with a maximum of £3,000 in cash and £1,000 in life insurance

or:

◆ up to three mini ISAs with up to £3,000 in one mini cash ISA, up to £3,000 in one mini shares ISA and up to £1,000 in a mini insurance ISA.

> **FACT:** You can't take out both a maxi ISA and a mini ISA in the same tax year, nor can you have two mini ISAs of the same type (such as two mini cash ISAs).

CASH TONE UP

Get the best deal

ISAs are offered by almost every bank and building society but you need to shop around for the best rates of interest. Use the Financial Services Authority's free, independent information to help you decide. Find these online at: www.fsa.gov.uk/consumer/compare

The ISA rules allow you to make withdrawals without losing the tax relief. But once you've deposited the maximum £3,000 allowance into the account in a tax year, you can't put in any more money in the account that year, regardless of how much you've withdrawn.

Activity

Wise up to ISAs

- You may not need – or be able to afford – an ISA now but make sure you understand how they work. Consider them when you're comparing savings schemes and accounts.

TOP TIP

- Don't forget that it's a case of 'use it or lose it' with each year's ISA allowance. You can't use the allowance from a previous year, so make the most of your annual opportunity.

CASH TONE UP

Your notes

CHAPTER 6

CREDIT JUICE BAR

Use credit cards wisely

Despite the pitfalls we covered in the chapters on debt and spending, credit can still be a useful financial tool when you have discipline. Whether you're paying for a power lunch or power tools, nothing is more convenient than a credit card.

Of course, flexibility is one of the main benefits of a credit card. If you have an unexpectedly large purchase you can cover it with your card and settle up later. Plus, unlike traditional loans, the amount you pay on your credit card each month is flexible. Once you've made a minimum payment – usually 2 per cent of your balance – you can choose whether to pay off the full amount or carry some credit over, which will then be subject to interest. This means that the cost of expensive items such as a camera or computer can be spread over several installments. Of course, the most cost-effective way to use a credit card is by paying off the balance in full every month.

TOP TIP

♦ The arrival of American card issuers has prompted the UK market to offer better deals and fight for your custom with increasingly tempting offers, such as interest-free introductory periods, cashback and perks. Shop around for the best deal and spend within your means and you'll have an excellent way to borrow money sensibly over the short term.

Activity

Make sure your card works for you

Make sure your card works for you and not the other way round. It should be a flexible friend, not a burden. Weigh up the pros and cons:

Pros

- Make purchases quickly and easily in person, by telephone and online.

- Use your flexible friend all over the world for international credit.

- Borrowing money for short periods is free if you pay off your bill in full each month.

- Your card issuer will even pay you if you use a cashback card.

- You can benefit from insurance on your purchases and may enjoy perks such as free travel insurance.

Cons

- Failing to pay off your bill each month can make credit cards expensive and hard to control.

- Withdrawing cash on your card should be strictly for emergencies as this will attract even higher interest and fees.

- If you need to borrow a large amount for a longer period, then you could do this more cheaply with a personal loan or even by remortgaging.

- Take care to ensure your card isn't lost, stolen or used fraudulently.

CREDIT JUICE BAR

The main thing to look for when choosing your credit card or any kind of credit, including a loan, is the annual percentage rate or APR. This figure helps to give you an idea of the cost of credit because it's the amount of interest you'll pay on any debt.

The impact of APRs

All lenders have to tell you what their APR is before you sign an agreement. The amount will vary from lender to lender but because they must declare the rate upfront, it should make it easier to shop around and compare deals. So, for example, if you leave £500 of debt on your credit card for a year at an APR of 18.9 per cent, you'll end up paying an additional £94.49 to the card issuer in interest charges. Look for the lowest APR you can find but make sure it's not just an introductory offer that will shoot up after a short period.

 TOP TIP

♦ Your card issuer will be happy if you keep a large balance on your card and pay them interest. A loan may be a cheaper way to clear the debt but shop around for the right one.

Activity

Know how to spot the best deals

If you find a deal with a low APR, ask the following questions:

- Does the interest included in the APR vary, or is the rate fixed? If the rate is variable, your repayments could go up or go down. If the rate is fixed, your repayments will stay the same.

- Are there any charges that aren't included in the APR? This could include something like optional payment-protection insurance. If so, make sure you understand what they are and when you'd have to pay them. You may decide to get them removed from the agreement.

- What are the conditions of the loan or credit and do they suit you? For example, do you have a choice about how and where you make the repayments? If you suddenly have spare money, can you pay the loan off early and without penalties?

- Can you afford the monthly payments? A more expensive loan (with a higher APR) could have lower monthly payments if they're spread out over a longer period of time. That might suit you better if your budget is tight.

Paying attention to the headline APR is important but don't let it blind you to other fees, charges and costs that may be hidden in the small print of a credit deal.

Activity

Learn how to spot and avoid credit gremlins

- Annual credit card fees used to be very common but as plastic gained popularity the fees dropped away. However, some card issuers have re-introduced them, so look for one of the many cards offering good deals without annual fees. The fee may be disguised as a contribution towards services available to the card holder, such as discounts on hotels or hire cars. But are you sure the special offers outweigh the cost of the fee?

- Late payment and over-limit charges are relatively new on the credit card horizon. Imagine paying your balance off in full, missing the payment date by one day and finding that the subsequent late payment charge pushes you over your limit to yet another charge. Expect to pay around £20–25 for each. Avoid them by being clear about your payment date and meeting it in good time. Some banks take several days to transfer cash from your account to the card issuer, even though the cash disappears from your bank account as soon as you make the payment.

- Transaction and withdrawal fees when using your credit card abroad are increasingly common and often apply whether you clear your balance in full or not. Only a small number of cards don't charge these. You can avoid them by knowing what your card charges and taking travellers cheques and currency, or using a debit card to withdraw cash and make payments.

- 'Typical' rates can be used by lenders and card issuers in their promotional material or adverts but there's a catch – they don't have to offer the seductive low rate to everyone. Instead, they can decide to offer a much higher rate once they receive your application. When a typical rate is advertised, the borrower won't know the exact rate they'll get until they apply, making it difficult to shop around. The lender will run a credit check on them and offer a rate based on that. This is also known as 'pricing for risk'. Don't be afraid to decline the loan or card if the rate offered is too high.

You may think it's easy to track down the right credit card for you but there are a host of added extras beyond the interest rate that can make a big difference. These aren't the first things you look for, but if you find several deals that are very similar they could help you pick the best.

Activity

Know how credit extras can work for you

Find out what offers come with your existing card and whether you've taken advantage of them.

Make sure you consider the following extras when comparing credit cards:

- With most credit cards, if you go out shopping on the day after you receive this month's statement, then you'll not be billed for your purchases until the same time next month and payment won't be due until three to four weeks after that. This amounts to an interest-free period and, in most cases, this is 56 days but can be as short as 45 days or as long as 59 days. The longer the interest-free period, the better.

- Your card may also come with perks and freebies. Travel insurance is a particularly popular add-on and can cover anything from £25,000 to £250,000. But read the small print before you travel – don't just assume it will cover you for all destinations and activities or numerous trips. Depending upon your card issuer, you could enjoy Air Miles, discounts or gift vouchers.

- A number of cards also offer purchase protection on transactions worth more than a certain amount – usually between £25 and £50. This means that items bought are covered against loss, accidental damage and theft for the first 90 or 100 days after you've bought them.

FACT: When you're deciding whether or not to put a purchase costing £100 or more on your credit card, remember that if what you're buying turns out to be faulty and the retailer refuses to co-operate by replacing it or refunding your money, you can make a complaint to the card issuer. MasterCard or Visa will investigate the case on your behalf and if they consider your claim to be valid, they're in a position to force the supplier to comply, or provide compensation themselves, under the Consumer Credit Act.

The important thing is not to be seduced by the perks but to compare them only when you've found low-APR cards that are right for your type of spending.

CREDIT JUICE BAR

It's nice to think that there might be some cash rewards for managing your credit responsibly. Cashback credit cards give you an incentive to spend but their benefits are only worth having if you're among the half of all cardholders who pay off your credit card balance in full every month.

How cashback works

For every pound you spend, the credit card issuer will give you some money back, usually after 12 months. Every time you buy something you qualify for a small percentage of the price credited back to your account. It's like getting a discount every time you go shopping and, when used properly, makes spending on your credit card cheaper than using a debit card or even cash.

How much could you get?

The value of the percentage can vary depending on the issuer, but anything between 0.25 per cent and 2 per cent is offered. Over special periods such as Christmas, some credit cards have been known to offer double cash back. But remember, if you pay your bill late or carry some credit – even for one month – then the card will work against you. The standard APRs on these cards are usually very high and the interest will outweigh the benefits of the cashback if you slide into debt. But, as with all plastic, you need to keep your deal under review.

 TOP TIP

- Cashback rates vary enormously between card issuers. A great offer that made your card the leader of the pack may suddenly change to an also-ran as the amount of cashback is cutback. Even a tiny reduction in the percentage of cashback can radically reduce the benefits.

CREDIT JUICE BAR

Activity

Take the cashback test

It's tempting to grab the chance of free cash but, surprise, surprise, it's not as simple as that. If you can answer 'yes' to the following questions then you could be ready to apply for a cashback card:

● Do you pay off your entire balance every month, without fail?

● Do you always pay your bill on time?

If the answer to one or both of the above is 'no' then keep trying to improve your credit habits.

TOP TIP

◆ There are more than 40 cashback cards and over 70 loyalty cards available to consumers, so shop around for the one that offers the best deal for you. Compare and contrast using the free, independent listings online at Moneyfacts.co.uk.

CREDIT JUICE BAR

It may be tempting to flash a glittery gold or platinum credit card when you buy your next round of cocktails or a digital camera. But apart from the snob value, would you get anything else of value from a so-called premium card?

Can anyone have one?

Traditionally, they've only been available to those earning a minimum of £20,000 to £30,000 per year because that was seen as the threshold for better credit risk. Qualifying for a gold card is now easier, and most banks and card issuers may waive any minimum income requirement, particularly for existing customers.

What's the big deal?

The higher credit limits that gold and platinum cards typically offer are part of the attraction. Most also come with a seductive selection of perks. Travel insurance and payment protection are the most common but other offers include cashback, Air Miles, discounts on videos and CDs or free motoring services.

◎◄ TOP TIP

- 'You can get some excellent freebies,' says Melanie Stewart of independent financial data company Moneyfacts. 'But make sure you check the monthly charges and that you're getting competitive rates of interest.'

What to look out for

Watch out for the high interest rate that kicks in once any introductory period has finished – it could increase dramatically. Check out the interest-free period too. This is the time between purchases hitting your statement and the date payment is due. It can range between 45 and 59 days. The longer the interest-free period, the better.

Activity

Decide whether you should go for gold

The colour of your credit card, the image it has or the additional perks it may provide should be the last things on your list of must haves. If you're tempted, follow these dos and don'ts:

- Do shop around and compare premium and standard cards. Look for the lowest interest rate (APR) as a starting point.

- Do look carefully at annual fees and charges that cover the cost of the perks – they can be very high.

- Don't take on a premium card based on its image, freebies or perks.

- Don't forget to review your card deal every few months – you may find you can save money by switching to a different card.

- Don't just opt for the same card as a friend or apply because the offer came in the post.

Not everything your credit card issuer provides is good for your financial health.

How do cash advances work?

One of the fastest ways to throw your money away is to use your credit card to make withdrawals at the cashpoint – also known as a cash advance. You can withdraw cash using most credit cards provided you have a PIN, but instead of having an interest-free period of between 49 and 59 days before interest is charged, as you do with purchases, cash withdrawals attract interest immediately. It's also likely to be a much higher rate of interest than your purchase rate.

Cash withdrawals also incur a handling fee or service charge, which tends to be a percentage of the amount taken out and is usually around 1.5 per cent for each transaction, although some banks charge a flat fee as well as, or instead of, this.

What are credit cheques?

These are provided by your card issuer and look almost exactly the same as ordinary bank account cheques but are often slightly smaller. They can be used in the same way as traditional cheques, even in places where credit cards are not accepted. But they're not so much convenient cash as fool's gold ...

What makes them bad for you

Credit card cheques are usually charged at the same rate as cash withdrawals. You'll also pay an immediate handling charge of between 1–2 per cent plus a minimum fee of around £2 per cheque. With most lenders, you'll also be charged interest immediately. Use them abroad and costs will be added for currency conversion.

TOP TIP

◆ Be aware! The protection you get automatically with card purchases over £100 doesn't apply to purchases made with credit card cheques.

Activity

Avoid credit advances and cheques

● Avoid the need for cash advances by keeping your budget healthy, planning ahead and building up your rainy-day savings. It's particularly important to avoid credit card cash advances when you're overseas as these could cost even more.

● Contact your credit card company and ask them not to send you any credit cheques. It will avoid them going astray in the post or being stolen. If your card issuer sends you credit cheques, shred them and ask the company not to send any more.

In an ideal world, we'd all pay off our credit card balances every month. But for some people, the only way they can keep their head above water financially is to carry over some of their costs from one month to the next on a credit card.

Activity

Start clearing debt and looking at balance transfers

- If you're among the half of plastic users who carry over some costs, then your aim should be to reduce the debt as quickly as possible and be free of those hefty interest payments. In the meantime, there are lots of great deals around that allow you to pay less on your debt so you can clear it more quickly.

- One of the easiest ways to find a breathing space and reduce your credit card debt is to cut out the interest. There are dozens of cards available that allow you to transfer your balance to a 0 per cent rate for an introductory period or to a very low rate for the life of the balance. Log onto www.moneyfacts.co.uk to find independent listings of the best balance transfer cards. They provide all the details to help you spot the best deal for your needs.

Keep on your toes

It's all too easy to assume that the hot credit card deal you signed up for six or twelve months ago is still the best available. But many interest rates are variable and the amount you pay for an outstanding balance could increase without you realising. If you signed up to an introductory rate, get ready to move again when it expires.

TOP TIP

♦ The constant desire of card issuers to attract new customers means there's a good chance that a more competitive offer is available elsewhere.

What to watch out for

Avoid high APR on any purchases during and after the balance transfer. If you transfer to a card with the best or longest 0 per cent period, but it has a high APR for ongoing purchases, then use an alternative card for these. This also avoids your repayments being used to first pay off the credit you run up on purchases while your transferred balance remains untouched.

TOP TIP

♦ You can set up a direct debit to pay off your credit card balance in full every month. Not only will this avoid late payment worries, it will help you stick to an affordable amount of credit.

Activity

Find the best credit card

Before you choose your card you should think about why you want it and how you intend to use it. Answer the following questions to help you decide which card is best for you.

1   What do you want to use your card for?

- Just to buy things and not for credit at all – you pay off your balance in full every month.

- To spread the cost of spending over a number of months – I can reduce my balance steadily.

- To take advantage of special offers such as lower rates for balance transfers.

- For emergencies – as a standby to give me easy access to credit if and when I need it.

2   What are the most important features for you?

- The interest rates – for purchases or balance transfers.

- The length of the interest-free period for purchases – this can be from 49 to 59 days.

- Incentives and benefits such as cashback, rewards or loyalty points.

- Using your credit card when you're abroad.

Some cards may specialise in one or two of these areas or offer most or all of them. But once you know what you're looking for, it will be much easier to pick the right card and not be distracted.

Asking yourself the following questions may also help:

3 Will I always clear my bill in full each month?

If the answer is 'yes' then you should look into the benefits of a cashback credit card (these are covered in Step 42). If you answer 'no' then look for the lowest interest rates available and a long interest-free period for purchases.

4 Do I want to buy a number of large value items that I can pay off over the next six months (e.g. when furnishing a house)?

If the answer is 'yes', consider a card with a low, or 0 per cent, introductory rate for purchases. If you plan to keep credit on the card beyond the initial period then make sure you know what the standard rate will be – these can often be considerably higher.

5 Do I travel abroad often and rely on my credit card to cover my expenses while I'm away?

If the answer is 'yes', alongside the interest rate and the interest-free period you should also consider the fees for transactions in foreign currencies, which can vary between cards.

Used sensibly, your credit card can be your flexible friend. But how would you cope if there were sudden changes in your circumstances that affected your income and made it hard to pay off your credit card bill?

How does payment protection work?

Almost all card issuers give you the opportunity to take out credit card payment protection insurance (PPI). It's designed to cover you if you can't pay your monthly credit card payments due to accident, illness, disability or unemployment. It can provide peace of mind but it does-n't come cheap, and if you decide you need it make sure you shop around for the best deal. You don't have to take the PPI offered by your card issuer.

 TOP TIP

- If you can find a better deal elsewhere, you can take out cover with another firm for your existing credit card.

The pitfalls of PPI

It's crucial to be aware of the pitfalls of PPI. Reading the small print may be dull but it's essential if you want the right cover. Here's what to look out for:

- If you're claiming because of illness, the policy may pay out when you're too sick to do your job or specify that you need to be too sick to do any job.
- The policy may not start to pay out until you've been ill for two weeks or more.
- The cover usually lasts a year but could be less.

◆ Make sure you know whether the PPI covers your entire balance paid or just a percentage.

◆ Some card issuers may automatically add payment protection. Check your account and ask for it to be removed if you don't need it.

Activity

Do you need PPI?

Answer the following questions:

1 If you lost your job unexpectedly, would your credit card bill or existing balance become a burden that you wouldn't be able manage?

2 If you were injured or sick for so long that you had to take reduced pay or if you were on maternity leave, would you be able to manage your credit card bills?

If you answered 'yes' to these questions then PPI may ease your worries. You could avoid the need for cover if you're sure that someone else – a partner or parent, perhaps – would be able to cover your loan repayments if the worst should happen.

CREDIT JUICE BAR

It's almost impossible to buy anything in a high-street shop without being asked whether you would like a store card.

Very expensive debt

Most store cards have an interest rate of at least 10 per cent more than the most expensive credit cards. Carrying a balance on your store card is the quickest way to get into debt. For example, if you spend £500 on a typical store card charging 29.9 per cent APR and pay it off in 12 months, you would pay £120.29 in interest. However, spend the same amount on a credit card with ten months interest free for purchases, and you would only pay £9.06 in interest over the year – a saving of £111.23.

Resist temptation

Store cardholders are often tempted by benefits such as loyalty schemes, discounts, special preview evenings and early access to sale stock. But these are easily outweighed by the rip-off interest rates. It's best to avoid store cards completely – just say no every time you're asked, however persistent the salesperson is.

Activity

Just say no

There's never a good reason to have a store card. But if you already have one or are determined to, make sure you understand the dos and don'ts:

Don't

- Don't see a store card as an easy option – there are so many debit or credit cards available that would better suit your needs. You don't need to sign up to high-cost plastic.

- Do check what the APR on the store card is if you're still tempted to have one – especially if you don't plan to pay off your balance every month. A high APR could outweigh the benefits of an initial discount.

- Don't sign anything until you've considered it carefully – take the form away with you to think it through if you're uncertain.

Do

- Do pay whatever you owe as soon as you owe it. If you can't pay off the balance in full straight away, stop using the card. Then pay off as much as you can afford. You may get a discount by paying via direct debit.

- Better still, find another way to transfer or pay off the debt so that you shake off the ridiculous interest rate. Then cut up the card and cancel the account.

- Do check out more top tips on what to avoid on the website of the Office of Fair Trading at: www.oft.gov.uk.

CREDIT JUICE BAR

Having a wallet full of plastic may make you feel wealthy or secure but if you're not using the cards or, worse still, if you're abusing them, then it's far better to cut down on the number you keep. This will also reduce the risk of theft and fraud.

Activity

Credit card cutback

- Start with a clearout. Take time to go through all your credit and store cards. By now, you should be aware of all your debts and have a plan to pay them off as soon as possible.

- Make sure you know the interest rate – APR – for each card. If you think it'll take some time before you can afford to pay off the entire debt, then consider transferring the balance to a 0 per cent deal. It may seem silly to sign up for more cards as a way to cut back but in this way you could save money on interest while you pay off the debt.

- As covered in Step 45, it may not make financial sense to use a balance transfer card for purchases. So the next step is to weigh up the card you plan to use for purchases against the best on offer in the market. Chances are you could get better value for money by switching. So that's one card for purchases and a second if you have a transferred balance that you're paying off. But only one of these cards will be 'in use'.

Emergency plastic

Some people like to have an unused credit card for emergencies. This is only suitable if you can be absolutely sure that you won't be tempted to abuse it. A weekend in Paris or a new outfit doesn't constitute an emergency. Keep the '999' credit card in a secure place but review what it offers at least once a year to ensure that if you do need to use it, you're not facing sky-high interest or other gremlins.

> **FACT:** Don't forget: Once your streamlined card system is in place, cut up the old cards and cancel the contracts.

Personal loans are lump sums that can be borrowed from banks, building societies and specialist companies. The loan is usually arranged for a fixed period for amounts between £1,000 and £15,000. Interest can be fixed or varied and rates tend to fall between 6 per cent and 14 per cent, making them a more practical – and usually cheaper – alternative to credit cards.

The two main types of loan are secured and unsecured. But what's the difference?

Activity

Get to grips with secured loans

It's essential know the difference between secured and unsecured loans and how they work. This will mean that you can understand the level of risk attached to any money you borrow.

- Secured borrowing includes mortgages or other loans that are linked to your house or another major asset. The money you borrow is secured against the value of the property you own. Put simply, this means that if you fail to repay the secured loan (or your mortgage), then your home can be taken from you and sold to cover your debts, even if they're significantly smaller than the property's value.

- As with any loan, it's crucial to borrow only what you can afford to pay back. And it's essential to shop around for the best deal – and that may not be the one offered by your existing bank or that arrives as a 'pre-approved' offer. Don't wait until you're desperate for the money. Taking time to find the right loan could save you hundreds of pounds.

FACT: If you already have a mortgage it may be cheaper to add to the cost of your home loan rather than taking out a separate secured loan. Because the risk of a secured loan is weighted against you, this is often the cheapest way to borrow. But you'll also need to consider any costs associated with changing or increasing your mortgage to borrow more and it's crucial that you don't overstretch yourself or your mortgage.

Don't forget: Read paperwork carefully so that you know the level of risk attached to any loan.

TOP TIP

◆ Thinking of taking out a secured loan to pay off several unsecured loans? Be aware of the increased risk you're taking on and refresh your memory on consolidated loans by re-reading Steps 19 and 20 again.

No matter how carefully you plan and budget, there may come a time when you need to borrow money. Millions of personal loans are taken out every year for all sorts of reasons. If you don't wish to secure the loan against your property – or you don't own property – then unsecured loans are a popular way to borrow.

How unsecured loans work

As with credit cards, the key to the cost of your loan is determined by the annual percentage rate (APR), which relates to the interest you'll pay on the cash you borrow. The interest can be charged at a fixed or variable rate. Sticking to a fixed rate will help you work out how much you can afford to borrow and give you certainty about your monthly payments. For example, if you borrow £5,000 at a fixed APR of 9 per cent then you'll be paying £450 in interest each year, which is spread across your monthly payments. All lenders must show clearly what the APR rate for any loan is so borrowers can compare products and see the true rate of interest they'd pay.

Activity

How to get the best from unsecured loans

● Borrow only what you can afford, even if you're offered more.

● Aim to pay the money back in as short a time as possible, according to what you can afford.

● Lenders often give better APR rates if you borrow larger amounts or pay back over a longer period. But taking more time to pay off the loan may not be the best option. If you lost your job or faced other financial pressures, then a long-term debt would be an additional burden.

● Equally, if you can suddenly pay off the loan early, you may be charged a penalty of some of the interest.

TOP TIP

Top tips to borrowing the right way

◆ Shop around for different rates, comparing APRs, flexibility and penalties. You may find it helpful to have the opportunity to repay the loan early without penalties.

◆ Choose the loan that's best for your circumstances.

◆ Make sure loan protection isn't included if you don't need it.

◆ It may be dull but it pays to read the small print. Go over the details very carefully before you sign.

CREDIT JUICE BAR

More than six million personal loans are taken out each year and most come with the offer of loan protection – insurance that will cover some of your repayments in certain circumstances. As well as only borrowing what you can afford, it's important to consider how you would cope with the repayments if your circumstances suddenly changed, for example if you faced unemployment or illness that affected your income.

How does loan PPI work?

PPI is designed to work in two ways:

1 It will pay off your loan completely if you die or you're diagnosed with a major illness like cancer, a stroke or a heart attack.
2 It will also cover your loan repayments for a set period of time if you can't pay them because of accident, sickness or unemployment.

If you're claiming because of illness, most policies pay out when you're too sick to do your job, although some specify that you need to be too sick to do any job – an important difference. You'll usually need to be off sick for more than two weeks before the policy will kick in and then most policies cover loan repayments for up to five years. If you resign or get sacked, then the policy won't pay out. Policies do vary so it's important to read the small print carefully.

Activity

Decide whether loan PPI is right for you

- Loan insurance isn't compulsory but is expensive and could cost hundreds of pounds. If you think you may want the added security of payment protection insurance – or PPI – then read the small print first.

- Bear in mind that cover may only start after several months of unemployment or missed payments. Think about whether there's someone who could help with payments if the worst happened.

TOP TIP

- Cover may be automatically included in your loan – research shows that nine out of ten high-street lenders do this – but this doesn't mean you must have it. Think about your specific circumstances before you decide whether you need it. Check whether it's been added and ask for it to be removed if you don't need it.

CREDIT JUICE BAR

An overdraft can be attached to your bank account and provide flexibility for your cash flow by giving you access to an agreed amount of money if you need it. For instance, if your bank grants you a £1,000 overdraft, it could be useful if you have a cheque that's clearing just before pay day.

Most banks will automatically offer you some sort of authorised overdraft limit when you open an account or start to have a regular salary coming in. If not, you can apply at most banks over the telephone or online, and many will provide an immediate decision.

How much do they cost?

Of course, overdrafts are a form of borrowing and so you have to pay for the privilege. If you're £1,000 overdrawn every month for a year with a typical high-street bank, then it's likely to cost around £180 per year. Online banks may charge considerably less – around £80 per year.

Arrange it before you need it

Most bank accounts won't let you make cash withdrawals if your account is empty, but they may honour cheques that take you beyond your bank balance into an unauthorised overdraft.

If this happens, you'll be charged a much higher rate of interest – possibly double the usual overdraft rate – and perhaps a fee on top. The bank will probably write a letter to you, pointing out the unauthorised borrowing and impose an administrative charge of around £25 for the cost of sending it. The fees and charges may come out of your – already overdrawn – account straight away, putting you even deeper into the red. So if you think you're about to go unexpectedly overdrawn, call the bank. It's more likely to be sympathetic if you give some warning.

Activity

Get the most from an overdraft

- The most important thing is not to leave it to the last minute. It's essential to arrange the overdraft in advance.

- Affordability is also key. You may be offered far more than you can ever catch up with, but you should accept only what you know will give you breathing space when you need it.

- Today, talk to your bank or find a leaflet in a branch which will explain the overdraft options available.

- Try to get information from several banks to see whether you are getting a good deal and so you can factor-in the differences when comparing bank accounts.

TOP TIP

- Always shop around for the best deal. If you plan on making use of overdraft facilities you may find you can save money by switching to a different bank.

'A bank is a place that will lend you money if you can prove that you don't need it.' Bob Hope, actor and comedian

CREDIT JUICE BAR

As ever, when it comes to finding cash to buy a car, it pays to do your homework. It makes sense to save for the wheels you want, but if you feel like you'll never get there without some help, make sure you choose the right sort of finance.

Don't get carried away

Although it may be tempting to sign up for finance in the showroom, don't get carried away. Most new cars lose around 40 per cent of their value within the first year or 10,000 miles. Car dealers often push finance deals, but these can be a particularly bad move if you're buying a car when the market is slow. Negative equity applies to cars as well as property and many drivers have been left with a long finance deal, which leaves them paying out much more than the car is worth.

 TOP TIP

◆ You may find an ordinary personal loan works out cheaper than specialist car finance offered by a dealer – so shop around.

Understand finance deals for cars

The AA recommends that motorists should get at least three quotes for loans before signing on the dotted line for a car finance package. There are a variety of routes:

Deferred purchase plans

These are loans where you pay off the interest and a part of the capital, leaving the remainder of the money (between 30 per cent and 60 per cent of the capital) to be paid when the loan expires.

Personal contracts

These work in a similar way but are usually only offered by car dealers. You pay a deposit of at least 10 per cent of the car's value and the repayments are usually low because of something called a minimum guaranteed future value (MGFV), which is taken off the purchase price. The MGFV is what the car is worth when the deal ends, providing the driver has not exceeded mileage limits. When the deal finishes, the driver can keep the car and pay the MGFV, or take out a new loan. You're less likely to be rejected for a personal contract plan, as the finance is secured on the car, which can be repossessed.

Hire purchase

You pay a deposit of around 10–15 per cent of the car's value plus monthly payments. As with personal contracts, the finance is secured on the car and you only own the vehicle once you've made all the payments.

CREDIT JUICE BAR

Lots of shops and companies win your business by offering you credit to help you buy what you want. Everything from a fitted kitchen to a flat-screen TV can come with a credit deal. Some of them are interest-free (only charging interest if you don't pay it all off by the deadline), but most charge interest and the longer you take to pay it off, the more expensive what you're buying becomes. Also, if you run into trouble with making your payments, the retailer might be able to repossess the goods you've bought.

Avoid the expense

Many finance offers start at 15 per cent because retailers often overcharge, knowing it's easier for you to sign up in the shop. The obvious solution is to save up the cash first. But if you need to rely on credit, you should be able to find a much cheaper deal through a personal loan.

Extended warranties

Buy any kind of electrical or white goods, such as a TV, washing machine or fridge, and you'll be offered an extended warranty by the sales person who earns a lot of commission on them. Also known as service agreements, extended warranties usually pay for any repairs to your appliance or replace it, if anything goes wrong in a specified period. This normally runs for four years after the manufacturer's one-year guarantee finishes. Some also include protection against accidental damage or insurance against theft.

Extended warranties can cost up to 50 per cent of the purchase price of the appliance, and many are bought as an afterthought.

Activity

Weigh up your warranty options

Will an extended warranty save you money?

It depends on the following:

1 What's the likely cost of repairing your appliance?

   This will vary. An Office of Fair Trading survey found that the average washing machine repair was between £45 and £65, and the average TV repair between £35 and £55. So if you pay £150 for a five-year extended warranty on a £300 washing machine, your machine would need to break down around four times in years two to five before you gained anything. However, this is worked out using averages, so it could cost more or less to have your machine repaired.

2 What's the cost of a new appliance compared with the cost of an extended warranty?

   It may be cheaper to replace the appliance if it breaks down outside a manufacturer's guarantee period rather than buying an extended warranty.

Picture the scene: you've been with your other half for some time. Perhaps you live together or are thinking about it. You trust each other so why not take out joint credit if you need it for, say, new furniture or a holiday? Before you take the plunge, it's essential to understand the risks of joint credit.

Who pays?

You'll be jointly and individually liable for the money that you owe. This means that if your partner leaves you and refuses to pay their share, the bank or finance company can, and will, come after you for the whole debt, not just your share of it. This is what you agree to when you sign up to joint credit. So even if you trust your partner 100 per cent, you must still be prepared to pay 100 per cent of the money back if the worst happens. This applies to any credit agreements, loans, overdrafts, rent arrears on joint tenancies, arrears on joint mortgages, council-tax payments and water charges on properties that have been jointly occupied.

When are you liable?

The key thing is whether or not you signed a joint agreement. Generally speaking, you're not liable for your partner's, or anyone else's debts, unless you signed an agreement or acted as guarantor. The two main exceptions to this are council tax and water charges. It's worth noting that regardless of your marital status or even the terms of any divorce settlement, creditors will still pursue you both for outstanding debts in both your names, even if one of you agreed in writing to pay them off.

> **FACT:** Your partner's bad money habits could also have a lasting effect on your own credit record, as you'll discover in the next few steps.

Activity

Know the dos and don'ts of joint credit

Dos

- Do have honest and open discussions about money, long before you need to sign anything.

- Do make a plan about how much each of you'll pay. This is especially important if one of you earns more.

- Do get legal advice if you need to protect money or property that one of you brings to the partnership.

Don'ts

- Don't be tempted to borrow more than you can afford.

- Don't be talked into borrowing for someone else because they're refused credit.

Big brother may not be watching you but finance companies certainly are. Somewhere, there's at least one file with notes on the financial moves you make. It's your credit reference file – also known as your credit rating file or credit record.

What do credit agencies do?

Organisations that lend money through credit want to know whether you're a good risk – in other words, whether you're likely to pay the money back. So whenever you apply for any kind of credit, the paperwork you fill out will state that the credit card issuer or loan company will contact a credit reference agency to check your financial history and notify them that you've applied for new credit. By signing the form, you give them permission to access your credit rating files. When you consider that there are currently more than 100 million credit, debit, charge and storecards sloshing around Britain, it makes sense to have some kind of central point of information so that lenders can make responsible judgements.

Information exchange

These files are held by Britain's three credit reference agencies called Equifax, Experian and Callcredit. They collect millions of pieces of information every month. This is sent to them by financial institutions such as banks and credit card issuers. They will also get data from shops and commercial businesses that are licensed to offer consumer credit on anything from mobile phone deals and store cards to 'buy now, pay later' offers. The credit reference agencies don't make any judgements themselves about your credit-worthiness. They just help credit issuers and lenders to share information.

Activity

Explore financial websites

Set aside an hour to surf the internet and explore some websites that'll provide you with ongoing information, tools, product details or calculators. Once you've picked a few favourites, get into the habit of looking at them regularly to keep up to date and pick up tips.

Try:

- The Financial Services Authority – www.fsa.gov.uk

- Yahoo! UK and Ireland finance – www.yahoo.com

- Money Saving Expert Martin Lewis – www.moneysavingexpert.com

- Moneyfacts independent comparisons – www.moneyfacts.co.uk

- This is Money – www.thisismoney.co.uk

- Interactive Investor – www.iii.co.uk

- Consumer campaigners Which? – www.which.net

- Guardian newspaper money section – www.guardian.co.uk

- Bradford & Bingley – www.bradford-bingley.co.uk

Compiled from credit applications you've filled out, your file will typically contain your current address, recent previous addresses and confirmation that your name and current address appear on the electoral roll, which allows you to vote. It also includes your date of birth and current and previous employers.

Credit details

The bulk of the report consists of details about credit accounts that were opened in your name or that list you as an authorised user (such as a spouse's credit card). Account details, which are supplied by creditors with whom you have an account, include the date the account was opened, the credit limit or amount of the loan, the payment terms, the balance, and a history that shows whether or not you've paid the account on time. Closed or inactive accounts, depending on the manner in which they were paid, stay on your report for up to six years from the date of their last activity.

Footprints

Credit reference agencies record an inquiry whenever your credit report is shown to another party, such as a lender, service provider, landlord or insurer. Inquiries – also known as footprints – remain on your credit report for up to two years. There'll be a note of your past and present applications for loans and credit (and whether or not they were successful) plus a record of any history of missed or late payments for loans and credit.

Problem pages

Additionally, the file contains information about arrears, defaults, county court judgements and bankruptcy. These are matters of public record obtained from government sources such as courts of law. Most public record information stays on your credit report for six years.

There are other problems that could haunt your credit rating file. Credit referencing will take note of anyone with whom you share joint credit, including mortgages. So, if your partner has had, or still has, financial problems, the negative associations could affect your credit score, even if you have an exemplary history.

Activity

Take note

- Grab a small, ruled notebook and keep it handy at work, at home or in your handbag. Use it to make notes on any thoughts and ideas you have or offers you spot which could help you manage your money more effectively. It will become your personal money manual.

CREDIT JUICE BAR

The information in your credit rating file is not just very personal: it affects your financial life and your ability to get credit. So it's essential that you get hold of a copy of each file to ensure the information held about you is accurate. It can also help you identify any issues that may prevent you from getting credit.

Black marks?

One million people per year apply to see their files. And because some lenders only use one credit reference agency or supply varying levels of detail, it's important to get your credit file from each of the three agencies to make sure that you're not being hampered by the black marks destined for someone else, possibly with a similar name, or penalised for applications or defaults that have never occurred.

Getting your file

To get copies of your credit files, log on to the credit reference agency websites for further information. The minimum fee is £2 but there are various online packages allowing you ongoing access to your file over longer periods, which will help you to keep a closer eye on your rating. If you don't have a credit card or can't afford to pay for an online service then you can apply for your file by post.

When asking for your file by post, you'll need to print off the application forms provided online by the agencies and enclose a fee by cheque or postal order.

 TOP TIP

- Remember, it's best to apply for all records as the agencies may have been given different information. It's worth getting copies of your files around twice a year to ensure they're accurate.

Statutory rights

The law restricts who has access to your sensitive credit information and what uses can be made of it. Your statutory rights include the right to:

◆ be posted a copy of your statutory credit report within seven working days of the request being received and payment made
◆ dispute inaccurate information
◆ have errors corrected within 28 days.

Activity

Get your mitts on your credit files

Britain's three credit reference agencies:

Equifax: www.equifax.co.uk
Credit File Advice Centre
PO Box 1140
Bradford
BD1 5US

Experian: www.experian.com
PO Box 9000
Nottingham NG80 7WP

Call Credit: www.callcredit.co.uk
Consumer Services Team
Callcredit plc
PO Box 491
Leeds LS3 1WZ

CREDIT JUICE BAR

Research shows that almost a quarter of people aged between 18 and 65 would have any credit applications rejected by UK banks and building societies. It's thought that this happens because of automated credit scoring techniques used by lenders. Many people whose credit applications are rejected then turn to unauthorised lenders and face interest charges of up to 300 per cent.

Trade secrets

What makes one credit company refuse you and another accept you? Of course the lenders aren't keen to share their credit scoring criteria with the public and rating techniques can vary enormously between one lender and another. Once they get your information from the credit reference agencies, some look for one or two pieces of basic information. For instance, if you're not on the electoral roll, then the credit company will believe there's a chance that your address isn't permanent, or – worse still – fake. This means that the company has no way of finding you if you're late with payments or will run up your credit limit and disappear. After all, who wants to lend money to someone they may not be able to find?

TOP TIP

♦ Even a high salary is no guarantee of getting credit – earning a six-figure sum is unlikely to make a difference if you're not on the electoral roll. Getting copies of your files will enable you to spot crucial gaps like this and rectify them.

Why don't they want you?

Switching balances and cards every few months has become common practice in the UK and some lenders may take a dim view of so-called 'rate tarts'. But sometimes, you can't win either way. Too little or non-existent credit can be just as much of a problem. Generally, unless you have any obvious financial horrors such as bankruptcy, you should be half way there if you appear on the electoral roll.

Activity

Healthy credit checklist

Make sure your credit chances are healthy.

I'm on the electoral roll.	
I've been registered on the electoral roll in every previous address.	
I pay my credit bills on time.	
I don't have any arrears.	
I'm in full-time employment.	
I've been with my employer for more than one year.	
I don't have any county court judgments.	

If the details on your credit reference file are correct you can't expect the agency to remove them just because they may be embarrassing. But you can ask for your file to be amended if the information on your file is incorrect or relates to other people with whom you've no financial connection.

Ask for a disassociation

If there's information on your file about people in your family with whom you have no financial connection, you can write to the agency to 'disassociate' yourself from them.

Activity

Sort out errors

Check your files for errors and if you find any, follow them up. There are three steps you can take if you have incorrect information on your file:

1 Write to the credit reference agency asking them either to remove or change any entry that you think is wrong. Explain why you think the information is wrong and send any evidence you have that proves the information is incorrect. The agency has to tell you within 28 days of receiving your letter if the information has been corrected, removed or if they have done nothing. If the information has been corrected, you'll get a copy of the new entry.

2   If the agency doesn't reply, or tells you they've done nothing or makes a correction that you don't think is satisfactory, you can, within 28 days, send them a 'notice of correction' to be added to your file. A notice of correction is a statement of up to 200 words written by you. It should explain clearly why you think the information is wrong or misleading.

3   If the agency doesn't reply to your letter enclosing your notice of correction within 28 days of receiving it, or the agency has refused to add it to your file, you can appeal to the Information Commissioner. The Commissioner works for the government and is responsible for enforcing the Data Protection Act. This protects people against abuse of any information that's held on computers.

You can find out more on the website:

www.informationcommissioner.gov.uk.

Or contact via post:

The Information Commissioner
Wycliffe HouseWater Lane
Wilmslow
Cheshire SK9 5AF

If you find your applications are being turned down, avoid going from lender to lender hoping to be accepted – it could make things worse by adding too many negative footprints on your credit files.

What's the cause?

There could be a good reason for your credit problems. If you have late or missed payments, loan defaults or county court judgements (CCJs) these may prompt a lender to decline your application for credit. If your debts are in the past but you're still struggling to borrow, there are ways to repair your dented record.

 TOP TIP

♦ Resist the urge to try to make everything better overnight and throw good money after bad. Credit repair companies can charge anything from £50 to £200 but there's nothing they do that you can't do yourself.

Make positive changes

♦ Start by getting a copy of your credit rating files from the three credit reference agencies. This should highlight any debt problems or errors.
♦ If you've taken steps to resolve debt problems but are refused credit, ask why. It might be that the credit scoring procedures used by a particular lender are very strict.
♦ The good news is that taking out some form of credit and then successfully meeting the repayments can help rehabilitate your credit status.
♦ Credit reference agency Equifax confirms that scores automatically improve as one's overall credit picture gets better. This means showing a pattern over time of paying your bills on time and using credit conservatively.

◆ You should focus on the red and amber warnings in your credit analysis provided with your file. These represent the main areas where you're not receiving maximum points.

Activity

Use this credit first aid checklist

- Pay your bills on time. ☐

- If you've missed payments, get up to date and stay up to date. ☐

- If you're having trouble making ends meet, contact your creditors or see a legitimate credit counsellor. ☐

- Pay off debt rather than move it around. ☐

- Re-establish your credit history if you've had problems. Opening new accounts and paying them off on time will raise your score in the long term. ☐

- Apply for and open new credit accounts only as needed. ☐

Many borrowers have access to too much credit: around eight million people in the UK are considered to be a high risk by lenders. Their income, credit rating or both will be too low for them to qualify for most types of loans or credit cards. But a whole world of alternative credit is opening up for those who are prepared to pay for it.

The 'sub prime' market

The 'sub-prime' market deals with people who don't qualify for most loans or credit cards. Lenders typically charge far higher interest rates on these loans for higher risk borrowers than on mainstream credit products, arguing that this is to cover the increased risk of customers defaulting on the loan. But there's no shortage of takers and as the demand for standard cards and loans reaches saturation point, many companies are considering expanding their range of financial products to cater for so-called 'sub-prime' customers who may have been refused credit in the past.

Help is at hand

High-street banks and building societies already cater for low earners who want basic bank accounts into which state benefits can be paid. There are now specialist mortgage lenders offering products to suit different levels of adverse credit and lending risk. Interest rates are likely to be higher than mainstream deals and brokers earn higher fees for selling sub-prime mortgages. Watch out – you could find specialist sub-prime credit cards ruinously expensive with rates on offer of up to 60 per cent interest. These cards usually have restricted credit limits to prevent you from running up endless debt.

 TOP TIP

- ◆ Make sure you read the terms and conditions of sub-prime products carefully to understand concepts such as compound interest, which is charged not only on the original debt but also on the interest charges that have stacked up so far.

Consumer campaigner advice

Sub-prime products and their lenders aren't without opposition. The National Consumer Council (NCC) has complained to regulators about high charges and poor choice. The debt-management charity the Consumer Credit Counselling Service urges borrowers to exhaust prime lenders before considering going to a sub-prime provider.

Activity — Are you on track?

Are you:

- saving statements and receipts? ☐
- shredding sensitive information? ☐
- banking online? ☐
- sticking to budget? ☐
- avoiding toxic spending? ☐
- using shopping lists? ☐
- tackling debts? ☐
- making savings? ☐
- using more cash than credit? ☐
- comparing, switching and saving? ☐
- understanding credit? ☐

CREDIT JUICE BAR

Phew. By this stage, your finances should be 'feeling the burn' of the substantial workout they've already had. Some of the activities you've already completed will take more getting used to than others.

New challenges

Taking a closer look at your budget is tough – particularly if you know that it's not likely to be very healthy. Taking steps to face reality and change your money habits will make everything that much easier.

Hang in there

Cutting out unnecessary spending could mean a significant change in lifestyle. It could be hard-going initially but once the benefits – more cash, more control and more choice – begin to show, your efforts will be rewarded.

Save a small fortune

Of course, reviewing your credit deals and delving into small print is not most people's idea of fun. But spending a few minutes on the detail will save you money and stop the lenders and card issuers having it their own way. Keep them on their toes.

Activity

See how far you've come already

Use today to take stock of all your progress so far and iron out any problem areas. If you've slipped a little on spending or debt then review your budget and work out how to get back on track. This could involve cutting back a little this month or next. If you can already see savings then resist the urge to spend them – there are lots of ideas still to come.

Over the next few days we will look at all sorts of ideas for making your money work harder, giving you a sound financial foundation for years to come.

Your notes

CHAPTER 7

LONG-TERM HEALTH

Life is full of dreams and goals and getting into financial shape will help you reach them.

TOP TIP

◆ Think about how long you can afford to tie up your cash. If you don't need instant access then you can earn more interest. Just remember to make a note of any notice you have to provide for withdrawals.

Activity

Make a savings plan

Follow these tips to make a plan for each of your goals or targets.

Be clear about your disposable income

Your healthy new budget will enable you to spot short-term demands on your money such as a big bill for car insurance.

Focus on your goals

Now make a list of the mid- to long-term goals that will need some cash. This may include a holiday, perhaps even a round-the-world trip. It may be your wedding, a new car or the deposit for a house or flat. List the goals or events in the order that you would like, or expect them, to happen and then, taking them one at a time, think about how much each is likely to cost. Work out how much you need to put aside each month and save a bit extra on top in case prices increase.

LONG-TERM HEALTH

Plan ahead and manage the cost

If something – such as a wedding or trip – is set for a specific time, planning will also help you spot whether you're going to have enough cash in time. This will give you a chance to plan any cutbacks, change the timing or boost your income in the meantime. It may be that you've been too ambitious and need to lower your expectations. Avoid loans and credit – only use them as a last resort.

Be disciplined

Once you know how much you can afford to set aside, avoid the temptation of spending the money and set up a special savings account. You can arrange a direct debit to move the money across just after pay day so that you don't miss it.

Premium Bonds are an investment where, instead of interest payments, investors have the chance to win tax-free prizes.

How Premium Bonds work

When someone invests in Premium Bonds they're allocated a series of numbers, one for each £1 invested. The minimum purchase is £100 (or £50 when you buy by monthly standing order), which provides 100 bond numbers and 100 chances of winning a prize. You can hold up to £30,000 worth of Premium Bonds.

ERNIE and prizes

Every month the winning bond numbers are generated randomly by a machine called ERNIE (electronic random number indicator equipment). Because ERNIE produces the numbers entirely at random, each individual bond has a separate and equal chance of winning a prize, regardless of when, where and how it was bought. In July 2004, the winner of the £1 million jackpot had just £17 in Premium Bonds, which were bought in 1959, and nine of the last 12 jackpot winners held less than the £30,000 maximum. The more bonds held, the better the chances of winning, but this doesn't mean prizes are won exclusively by higher-value holdings.

As well as two £1 million jackpots you can win anything from £50 to £100,000 for each bond number you hold every month. Any prize you receive is free of UK income tax and capital gains tax. Of course this compensates for the fact that your money doesn't earn interest and isn't protected from inflation. But the pros outweigh the cons.

> **FACT:** You can cash in all or part of your bonds at any time. Expect to receive your money back within about a fortnight.

100 per cent risk-free

One of the biggest attractions is that any money you invest in premium bonds is 100 per cent secure. Only National Savings and Investments can make this promise because their investments are backed by HM Treasury.

Activity

Get to grips with Premium Bonds

Now you know how they work, think carefully about whether Premium Bonds may make a good short- or long-term home for some of your savings:

- Remember that your money is protected but won't earn interest.

- The minimum investment is £100 but it could win you a million.

- You can buy Premium Bonds from your local post office or by post from National Savings & Investments (NS&I).

- You can also download an application form from the NS&I website at: www.nsandi.com or phone 0845 964 5000 to ask for one.

As we discovered in Step 37, mini – or cash - Individual Savings Accounts (ISAs) are versatile ways to save over the short-, medium- or longer-term.

How maxi ISAs work

Maxi ISAs provide a chance to invest your money in larger amounts. You can choose to invest up to £3,000 in cash, up to £1,000 in life insurance and the remainder in stocks and shares – or put your full £7,000 in the stocks and shares component. Maxi ISAs must have a stocks and shares component and many investors choose to invest the entire annual ISA allowance in stocks and shares. But the current rules are that that you can't, at some future point when your circumstances change, switch components (e.g. changing your stocks and shares holdings into cash or insurance or vice versa).

The components

The stocks and shares component of your ISA can include individual shares listed on any recognised stock exchange, gilts (fixed rate bonds issued and guaranteed by the UK government), corporate bonds, unit trusts, open-ended investment companies (OEICs) and investment trusts.

The cash component is the most straightforward and can include bank and building society deposit accounts, cash unit trusts, money market funds and any National Savings products, except savings certificates and Premium Bonds.

The life insurance component isn't offered by as many providers as the other two components. It's important to remember that the life product inside the ISA wrapper is intended for savings rather than to provide cover.

It's worth noting that not all providers will offer the range of components that you want. Check before you sign up.

> **FACT**: Remember, you can't take out a mini ISA and a maxi ISA in the same tax year. Nor can you take out more than one mini ISA of the same type in the same tax year. And don't forget that the allowances are annual and you can't go back and make use of years that you've missed. Each year is a one-off opportunity.

Activity

Knowledge review

Today has given you a basic understanding of maxi ISAs. Tick off the following facts that you should have learnt:

- More money can be invested in maxi ISAs – up to £7,000 in 2005/6. ☐

- Maxi ISAs must have a stocks and shares component and you can invest the whole £7,000 in them if you choose. ☐

- You can't take out a mini ISA and maxi ISA in the same tax year. ☐

LONG-TERM HEALTH

Before opting for the most convenient investment account or scheme, make sure you understand and feel comfortable with the level of risk, if any, that your money will be exposed to.

While deposit accounts are ideal for low-risk, shorter-term savings, you can get better returns over a longer period of time through stock-market-based investments. But where there's the potential for reward, there's also risk. Investments based on stock-market performance may offer the potential of higher returns when the market's good, but the flip side is that your money may not grow at all and you may not even get all your original investment back. Before you take the plunge, make sure you understand and feel comfortable with the risk involved in your choice of investment. For instance, are you guaranteed to get back at least what you put in?

FACT:
- Because investments are often complex and carry some risk, it's important to get a qualified, authorised professional to help you before you part with your cash. There's no quick or easy way to get rich quick on the stock market. It pays to be suspicious if you're offered the chance to invest in a scheme that promises huge returns on your money. Don't be rushed into anything and make sure you take the time to check whether the scheme's legitimate. If something appears too good to be true, it probably is.
- Put simply, buying a share means you own part of a company. When the stock market's doing well and shares in your company are in demand, you could see your investment grow substantially. When times are tough, the value of your company – and therefore the shares in it – will decrease and make your investment worth less. This is the key thing to remember about buying share-based investments – your money is at risk. You should also be prepared to invest money for the long term as the ups and downs of the stock market over the short term could eat into the cash, whereas sharp falls and rises tend to even out over the longer term.

Activity

Are you ready to ride the stock market?

How familiar are you with the risks involved in the stock market? Answer 'true' or 'false' to these statements (answers below).

	True	False
The stock market stays stable for 2 years at a time.		
Deposit accounts are lower risk than investments.		
There is always risk with shares and investments.		
You can buy shares from anyone who wants to sell them.		

Shares form the basis of so many investments, including pensions. It's important to know the pros and cons even if you are not ready to invest yet.

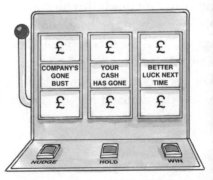

Answers: false, true, true, false

You don't have to buy shares directly to give your money a run on the stock market. There are lots of plans and products available that arrange the investment for you and can help spread the risk.

TOP TIP

- Before you hand over your cash, make sure you know how a scheme works and what risks are involved.

Collective investments

If you feel nervous about going it alone, then a collective investment will provide stock-market exposure but the risk will be shared with other investors. It's a general term that includes share-based, professionally run products such as unit trusts, investment trusts and Oeics (open-ended investment companies). You can make regular contributions and your money is pooled with that of other investors and invested in a wide range of companies, spreading and sharing the risk.

Unit trusts

Unit trusts are funds that also invest in the shares of other companies. You buy units in the trust and your money is then pooled with other investors to buy shares, with the risk spread across many different companies and markets. The future price of your units is dependent upon the value of the overall portfolio that the manager is running and not the demand for the units in the trust itself.

Investment trusts

Investment trusts are companies that invest in the shares of other companies. The investment tends to be widely spread, which reduces the risk to the investor. The price of your share is determined by the demand for shares in this specific investment trust company, as well as the underlying value of its investments.

Open-ended investment companies

Oeics are similar to a unit trust in that the number of units increase or decrease according to demand. However, like an investment trust, the investment is held in a company and units are bought or sold at a single price.

Investment bonds

Investment bonds are one-off lump sum investments as opposed to regular savings plans and are primarily designed to be medium- to long-term investments. The eventual return you receive depends on the movement in the unit prices over the period of the policy.

Activity

Feel ready to invest

- Understanding investment products and the risks attached is a big step towards making your money work harder. You also need to be ready to invest. If you have any remaining doubts then keep asking your financial advisor questions until you feel comfortable.

LONG-TERM HEALTH

If money is tight and you're juggling bills, paying off debts or trying to save, it can be almost impossible to think about buying a property. With average house prices increasing faster than average pay, around a third of all homes in Britain are rented. If you're trying to decide whether to rent or buy, consider these pros and cons.

The advantages of renting

◆ Renting is generally cheaper. The Association of Residential Lettings Agents says a £178,000 apartment will rent out for £800 a month whereas a 25-year standard variable-rate mortgage on the same apartment would set you back around £952 a month.
◆ It may be the affordable option. Rather than overstretch your finances if you're not ready for a mortgage, you can rent while saving for your deposit.
◆ Having a landlord means that someone else is responsible if the boiler breaks down.
◆ You don't have to pay the start-up costs associated with buying, such as mortgage fees, surveys and new furnishings.

If you're at a stage in your career where relocation may be on the cards, the flexibility of renting rather than buying may appeal.

The advantages of buying

◆ You're investing in an asset rather than helping someone else to pay off their mortgage with your rent.

◆ You're on the property ladder and have a chance to improve your home and sell it at a profit further down the line.

◆ The property is yours and you can do what you like to it and in it.

◆ There is no deposit payable to a landlord who may then only refund it after a debate about the way the property has been left.

◆ You don't have to deal with any landlords or flatmates, decor you don't like or the hassle of chasing someone else to arrange or pay for repairs.

Activity
Weigh up the pros and cons

● Now you know the upsides and downsides of both renting and buying, it should be easier for you to see which would suit your finances right now. Renting may be more realistic if money's tight. Buying and owning is a big commitment but you can be king or queen of all you survey.

LONG-TERM HEALTH

Whether it's with a girlfriend, boyfriend or flatmate, living together can be great fun but can also bring potential headaches – and not just about who has the remote control. Regardless of how long you've known each other and who pays for what, there's no legal protection and if your friendship ends in tears, there are no guarantees about happy financial endings.

Living together agreement

Britain's two million co-habiting couples are now being urged to take stock and complete a living together agreement. This government-backed document is similar to pre-nuptial agreements and is already popular in America. It addresses questions about individual earnings, who owns what and how household bills will be paid. While not legally binding, it could be brought up in any court proceedings. There is also the option to give it greater formality by asking a solicitor to write it up as a deed, making it legally binding in the same way as any legal contract between two parties.

Common sense

A living together agreement isn't just there incase you split up – it's a common sense way of organising the day-to-day arrangements of living together and protect both parties from whatever might happen in the future, including the possibility of the death of one of you. Making the agreement prompts you to discuss how living together will work in practice and what your expectations of each other are.

Cover the basics

An agreement will help you to organise the day-to-day finances of living together, which could be particularly tricky if one of you earns more than the other. It prompts you to think about easy and fair ways to divide the costs, and avoids those niggling little arguments about who's paying for the food, and who's paying the gas bill.

TOP TIP

♦ Find out more about the financial implications of co-habiting on the website: www.advicenow.org.uk.

Activity
Take the living together test

Put 'true' or 'false' beside the following:

I've been living with my other half for more than two years so we have the same rights as a married couple. ....

His/her name is on the property deeds but I pay half the mortgage so we own jointly. ....

If we split up I'd automatically get half of everything. ....

The answer to all three questions is 'false'. How did you score?

LONG-TERM HEALTH

Short of a lottery win, the only way most people can afford to buy a home is by borrowing some or most of the money. Most buyers must put down a deposit – a sum of money, which is usually at least 5 per cent of the property's value but more often between 10 and 25 per cent.

TOP TIP

◆ Fees and freebies usually come with mortgage deals. The lender will charge an arrangement fee for the administrative work but may offer free valuations, insurance or legal fees. Make sure you choose the deal that is best for you and do not get seduced by freebies.

There are two main ways you can repay your home loan. Choose between a traditional repayment mortgage or an interest-only mortgage. Here's how they work.

Repayment mortgage

Many homebuyers like the simplicity of the repayment option. Every monthly payment you make reduces the interest on the loan and some of the capital (the amount borrowed) until the entire loan is paid off by the due date. This steady and reliable approach makes the repayment option low risk and so it appeals to borrowers who want the absolute security of knowing their mortgage will be paid off by a certain date.

Interest-only mortgage

As the name suggests, with an interest-only mortgage your monthly payments are smaller and cover just the interest on the loan. At the same time, you make regular contributions to separate investment or savings schemes such as an individual savings account (ISA) with the expectation that it will produce a large enough lump sum to pay off the capital you still owe at the end of the mortgage term – usually 25 years.

There is risk attached to this type of mortgage. An investment dependant on stock-market performance may go down as well as up and you'll have to make up any shortfalls before the end of their mortgage term.

The uncertainty attached to this type of repayment method means it tends to suit borrowers who are prepared to accept some risk. It also means you have to trust yourself to keep your mitts off the investment and not dip into it.

TOP TIP

♦ As your lifestyle and appetite for risk changes, you may decide to switch from a repayment mortgage to an interest-only loan or vice versa. This can usually be done fairly cheaply and easily and can help you adjust the size of your monthly payments for a while if you need to.

Activity

Which type are you?

● Think about the level of risk you're comfortable with and how much self-discipline you have when choosing the best mortgage for you.

LONG-TERM HEALTH

When property prices increase, it's great news for existing homeowners but makes life harder for first-time buyers. Mortgage lenders understand this and a wide range of products is available to help you afford your first home.

100 per cent mortgage

Paying a deposit of 20 or 25 per cent of the cost of the property will probably help you secure a more competitive mortgage deal as loans of less than 80 per cent of the property's value tend to attract lower interest rates and fewer fees. However, with rent and bills to pay more people are finding it hard to save quickly enough. One alternative is a 100 per cent mortgage. The rates are usually slightly higher and if property prices drop, you could immediately find you have negative equity – where your mortgage is higher than your property value. These deals also tend to attract a Mortgage Indemnity Guarantee (covered in Step 76).

Guarantor mortgage

If your income is too low and you worry about over-committing yourself, your parents may be able to help with a lump sum. Alternatively, some lenders offer special deals where your parents can agree to assist if there are any payment difficulties. These are called guarantor mortgages. Most lenders ask the parent to guarantee the entire loan, but some only ask them to be guarantor for the element outside the amount their child can afford.

LONG-TERM HEALTH

Buying with a friend

If you move in with a friend you should find it much easier to buy with two incomes. But make sure the legal status is clear should either of you wish to sell. Try renting together first to make sure you get on. Alternatively, buy on your own but allow friends to help pay the mortgage using the Inland Revenue's Rent a Room scheme. This allows a certain amount of the income to be received tax-free from rental of furnished accommodation in your only or main home. Special mortgages are also available that allow borrowers to add the rental income from letting one room onto their salary before their income multiples are assessed. Talk to mortgage lenders and shop around for the deal that suits you best.

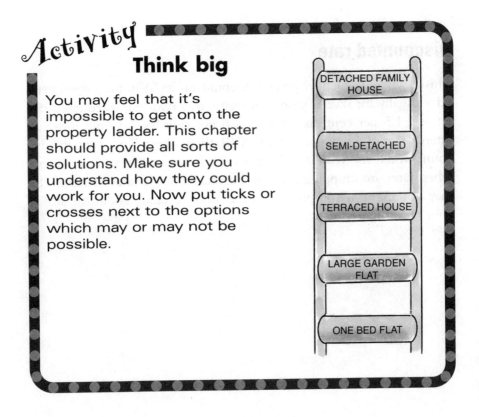

Activity Think big

You may feel that it's impossible to get onto the property ladder. This chapter should provide all sorts of solutions. Make sure you understand how they could work for you. Now put ticks or crosses next to the options which may or may not be possible.

DETACHED FAMILY HOUSE

SEMI-DETACHED

TERRACED HOUSE

LARGE GARDEN FLAT

ONE BED FLAT

LONG-TERM HEALTH

In the same way that you choose a way to repay your mortgage that's right for your circumstances, the type of mortgage interest rate you opt for should also reflect your financial goals. There are several options.

Standard variable rate (SVR) mortgage

All lenders have this standard rate that goes up and down as the lender adjusts it to economic and market conditions, and follows the Bank of England's base rate of interest. Although the SVR tends not to carry any restrictions or penalties, it's rarely the cheapest rate to be on. It may not suit those who want to pay a set amount every month and better value for money can almost always be found elsewhere.

Discounted rate

This is where the lender gives a discount on its SVR for a fixed period – usually for several years. For example, a two-year discounted rate set at a 1.5 per cent discount on a 6 per cent SVR would mean an interest rate of 4.5 per cent. If the SVR then rose to 7 per cent, the discount would rise with it to 5.5 per cent. Be aware that you can benefit when rates are dropping but will be caught out if rates increase. This may not appeal if you prefer to have more certainty about the size of your monthly payments.

Tracker rate mortgage

These have variable rates that move in line with the Bank of England's base rate of interest or the London inter-bank offered rate (LIBOR). Tracker rates are usually set for a fixed period slightly above the rate that they're following. This is good news when rates are dropping but climbing rates will be passed on to you as well, meaning you may sometimes need to increase your payments. Some lenders have a minimum rate on their tracker mortgages below which your rate won't fall – known as a collar.

TOP TIP

◆ You may be offered immediate cashback if you commit to an SVR or tracker rate for a set number of years (usually five). Remember you'll pay for the privilege through higher monthly payments on the SVR with no protection from rate increases.

Activity

Know how to choose the right mortgage

● Understand the choices and aim to find the lowest rate of interest that works in a way to suit your lifestyle and expectations. Be prepared to review your deal every couple of years.

LONG-TERM HEALTH

Fixed-rate mortgage

As the name suggests, the rate of interest is fixed for an agreed period – say, two, five or ten years. Fixed rate loans traditionally appeal to borrowers who like the certainty of a static monthly payment and don't want to risk an increase in their mortgage payments.

Remember, if base rates fall during the term of the deal, you could be tied in and won't benefit from the cuts. At the end of the fixed-rate period, borrowers will typically be converted to the lender's SVR and it will be time to switch. Beware of offers that lock you into the SVR for a further agreed period (from one to five years) once the fixed rate ends. These are called extended redemption tie-ins and are best avoided because there's almost always a cheaper rate to be found elsewhere.

 TOP TIP

♦ Your lender may not give you very much – if any – warning when your fixed-rate period is about to expire. It will be up to you to make a note of the relevant date and plan ahead.

Capped-rate mortgage

With a capped-rate deal you pay the SVR but your lender will set an upper rate – or cap. Your interest rate is guaranteed not to rise above this level for the period the cap is in place. This has an obvious advantage during times of high interest rates but capped deals aren't usually cheap. You can cap for anything from six months to five years. Again, make sure you know what penalties apply and avoid getting locked into the standard rate once the capped period is over.

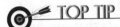

TOP TIP

◆ Avoid capped products where the cap is set so high that it's unlikely to be reached, even when rates are high.

Flexible mortgage

Some mortgages will penalise you for paying off larger amounts or lump sums. With a flexible mortgage you can alter your payments in line with your ability to pay either more or less than expected. These loans attract homeowners who may need to make smaller payments for a few months, for example, if they're stopping work to have a baby. You can also make larger payments or contribute lump sums, for example, from a bonus or inheritance.

Activity

Get to grips with more mortgages

● Don't be put off by all the new information – understanding the basics will be a huge help.

● All big mortgage lenders have helpful websites and easy-to-understand leaflets in branches.

● Start gathering guides and leaflets that can help boost and update your knowledge.

● Organise them into a file so the information will be at your fingertips.

LONG-TERM HEALTH

163

If life were simple, then all mortgages would do exactly what they said on the tin. Unfortunately, there are several hidden costs that can lurk around your home loan.

Mortgage indemnity guarantees (MIGs)

If you're borrowing more than around 90 per cent of the value of the property, the lender will probably require a mortgage indemnity guarantee or MIG. This single-premium insurance policy protects the lender – not you – if the property has to be repossessed and is sold for less than the outstanding mortgage. The cost will also be added to the mortgage so you'll pay interest on it.

Extended redemption penalties

Most mortgage deals have some kind of redemption penalty – the fee you must pay the lender if you decide to switch your mortgage early. Some have an extended redemption tie-in, which means you must stay with the lender for a certain period – usually several years – after the fixed- or capped-rate period has expired. Getting out of the deal altogether will come at a price.

Early repayment charges

You'd think that someone who's lent you a lot of money would be delighted to get some of it back more quickly than promised. Not your mortgage lender. Unless your home loan is flexible, you could face charges if you try to repay all or some of the debt early. You may be better off leaving extra cash in a high-interest account until you switch loans.

Compulsory insurance

Some lenders insist that you have to take out compulsory insurance policies as a condition of getting the loan. These may include buildings and/or contents insurance, or accident, sickness and unemployment insurance. Locking insurance into a mortgage deal is known in the trade as bundling and is seen as a purely money-making opportunity by lenders. You may not need the cover and could be overcharged by as much as 40 per cent. Avoid bundling and check what cover is offered by your employer.

Activity — Pit stop

You're making great progress through the steps now. If you had to score the improvement in your financial knowledge and skills, would it be:

0–3: I'm struggling

4–7: I'm managing

8–10: I'm a natural

If you scored less that 7 then write down the areas where you feel less confident and review the steps that will help build your confidence and competence.

TOP TIP

- ◆ The way the interest on your mortgage is calculated by the lender can also make a difference to what you pay. Look for interest calculated on a monthly or daily basis rather than annually.

LONG-TERM HEALTH

Keeping up-to-date with your mortgage is essential and so it comes as no surprise that many people opt to take out some sort of insurance. If you fall behind with your mortgage repayments and can't catch up again, you could eventually lose your home.

Mortgage payment protection insurance (MPPI)

How it works

Mortgage payment protection insurance (MPPI) covers your monthly mortgage payments for a specified period – typically one or two years – if you have an accident, become ill or unemployed. You pay a premium each month while the mortgage is running. If you lose your job, or can't work because of an accident or illness, the policy starts to pay out (usually directly to your lender) to cover your mortgage.

What it pays

To keep the cost of the insurance down, there are usually several exclusion periods so it's vital to check the individual policy for exact details. Payments are usually limited to a maximum amount of money – around £1,000 to £1,500 per month. There's an excess or waiting period of up to 60 days for each claim, during which no payments will be made. So it makes sense to try to keep enough money in savings to cover two months' worth of mortgage payments, even if you have MPPI.

 TOP TIP

- If you already have accident or sickness protection from your employer, income protection or critical illness insurance, or substantial savings, you may decide that you don't need MPPI insurance.

LONG-TERM HEALTH

Activity

Know how to weigh up the benefits of MPPI

Answer these questions.

1   If you lost your job unexpectedly, would your mortgage become a burden that you were unable to manage?

2   If you were injured or sick for so long that you had to take reduced pay, or if you were on maternity leave, would you be able to manage your mortgage payments?

If you answered 'yes' to these scenarios then MPPI may ease your worries. You could avoid the need for cover if you are sure that someone else – a partner or parent, perhaps – would be able to cover your loan repayments if the worst should happen.

Make sure you approach MPPI with your eyes open and don't sign up to something because you're distracted by the excitement of buying property. If you're taking out a new mortgage, you'll probably be offered MPPI. It's usually cheaper and the terms may be more generous if you take it out at the time you start your mortgage, rather than leaving it until you've had your mortgage running for a while.

Policies may be getting simpler, cheaper and more popular but look before you leap. Think carefully about your own circumstances and seek independent advice if you have any questions.

LONG-TERM HEALTH

It's very easy to put pensions at the very bottom of a long list of dull financial things that you don't think you need to worry about. That would be a big mistake.

Why pensions matter

Put simply, a pension is a retirement plan designed to provide a secure income for life when you stop working. You may ask why you need to bother with a pension. But it's unwise to rely on the state to provide you with enough to live on – the tiny state pension may not even exist by the time you retire.

What will you live on when you stop work?

We're living longer and healthier lives, so it's even more important to think about how and when to save for retirement. Retirement can last for 20 or 30 years or longer. Depending on how luxurious you want your retirement to be, you'll need to set aside cash now to fund everything from living costs to round-the-world cruise costs.

> **FACT:** The state pension is paid by the government and if it's still being paid when you retire, don't expect it to fund a life of luxury or even comfort. It's based on the National Insurance (NI) contributions you make during your lifetime. At the time of writing, it's worth just over £80 per week.

You're never too young

It's a myth that you can be too young to start a pension. The sooner you start saving, the better off you'll be when you need the cash because your pension savings need a chance to grow over time.

Activity

Work out how much to save in your pension

- Think about the lifestyle you'd like to have when you retire.

- Calculate how much you can afford to contribute towards your pension fund each month.

- You'll also need to take into account when you want to retire and whether you have income from other sources.

- Put away as much as you can afford as soon as you can.

- To provide additional encouragement, the government gives us a tax break on our pension savings.

TOP TIP

- Once you've set up a retirement plan, keep an eye on how your investments are growing (or not) and how well they suit your circumstances and plans.

LONG-TERM HEALTH

169

Many employers provide occupational or company pension schemes. If you're an employee and you can join an occupational pension scheme, you'll normally be better off doing so. This is because most employers who run occupational pension schemes contribute to the scheme themselves and some run schemes where you don't have to pay any money at all. Occupational pension schemes may also provide extra benefits such as a pension to your husband or wife when you die or a pension if you become ill and have to retire early. A pension scheme linked to your salary will also increase in line with your pay rises.

> **FACT:** Occupational pensions are usually very good value, so find out if your employer runs a scheme before you look into any other options.

How safe are company pensions?

Unfortunately, occupational pensions aren't completely risk-free. Some salary-related occupational schemes have been in the news because employers have closed them with insufficient funds to keep their pension promises, and some members of these schemes have lost some of their retirement benefits. According to financial regulator the Financial Services Authority, an employer can wind up a salary-related scheme at any time, if they can secure all the benefits. The government set up a Pension Protection Fund in April 2005 to protect members of salary-related schemes. The fund pays some compensation to scheme members whose employers become insolvent and where the scheme doesn't have sufficient funds to pay out members' benefits.

TOP TIP

◆ Occupational pension schemes may also provide extra benefits such as a pension to your husband or wife when you die or a pension if you become ill and have to retire early. A pension scheme linked to your salary will also increase in line with your pay rises.

Final salary schemes

Other occupational schemes that pay out a pension based on 'defined benefits' or the final salary of the employee have also been in the spotlight. These schemes are very generous and are often provided to public-sector workers to make up for the smaller salaries they earn. However, they're very expensive to run and many companies have decided to close their schemes to new employees as a result.

Activity

Find out more

● Talk to your employer for information about the available pension options that through your work.

'If women didn't exist, all the money in the world would have no meaning.' Aristotle Onassis, shipping magnate

LONG-TERM HEALTH

If you don't have access to a company pension via your employer to increase your retirement income, you should consider additional pension provision.

How personal pensions work

Personal pensions are also known as private pensions and can move with you from job to job. Some employers who don't run an occupational pension scheme may arrange for a personal pension provider to offer their employees a personal pension instead. Personal pensions arranged in this way are called group personal pensions. The charges may be lower because of the number of people involved, and the employer may also agree to pay extra contributions on top of what you pay in.

You usually pay into the personal pension directly from your salary every month. The money in your pension fund is invested to pay for a regular income when you're older. But you may also have to pay charges to your personal pension provider.

Tax relief

You'll usually get tax relief on your contributions to a personal pension, which is the government's way of encouraging you to pay into pension schemes. This tax relief is available to everyone who pays into a personal pension, even those who don't pay tax. The pension provider claims tax back from the government at the basic rate of 22 per cent. In practice, this means that for every £78 you pay into your pension, you end up with £100 in your pension pot (based on the tax year 2005/06). If you pay income tax at the higher rate of 40 per cent, you can claim back the tax difference (compared with the basic rate of income tax) from the Inland Revenue. So with the higher rate of income tax at 40 per cent, every £100 that goes into your pension fund costs you £60 (based on the tax year 2005/06).

What you get at the end

The money you pay into your pension fund is invested and grows throughout your working life. When you retire, you can take up to 25 per cent of your fund as a lump sum and the remainder must be used to buy something called an annuity, which pays you an income throughout your retirement.

Activity

Find out all you need to know

- Pensions are very important aspects of your finances but they're complex and not always easy to understand.

- Make sure you find out as much as possible about the best pension for you.

- If you're not sure what to do for the best, seek advice from an independent financial advisor.

LONG-TERM HEALTH

Just when you thought you were getting to grips with the basics of pensions, there's another type of scheme to consider.

What are they?

Stakeholder pensions were launched in 2001 and are simplified, cheaper versions of personal pensions. Providers can't charge anything other than an annual management fee, which is capped at 1 per cent, whereas many pension managers charge much more. The government introduced them because the basic state pension is unlikely to provide enough income for most people in their retirement. Employers who choose not to offer a company scheme must give employees access to a stakeholder pension scheme, although they don't have to contribute.

How do they work?

Stakeholder pensions are flexible. You can transfer to another scheme at no cost and there are no penalties for transferring money in or out, stopping and starting contributions, varying their size or retiring early. With a stakeholder scheme, individual contributions can be as little as £20, paid as irregularly as you like. There is also an upper limit on contributions. You can invest up to £3,600 (based on 2005/6 rules), or a set percentage of your earnings, depending on your age, in a stakeholder pension each year. This figure includes your own contributions, any contributions your employer may make and the tax relief you receive from the Inland Revenue.

Are they expensive?

Stakeholder pensions carry low charges and were designed for people who currently don't have access to an occupational pension or a good-value personal pension to save for their retirement – although they're open to anyone who wants one. They may interest you if you're self-employed, a lower earner or you don't have an income of your own but can afford to save for a pension.

LONG-TERM HEALTH

174

⊙⤙ TOP TIP

◆ Don't forget: As with all pensions, you should compare stakeholder pensions with the other pension options available so you can make an informed decision about which option is best for you. For instance, if your employer runs an occupational scheme, it will normally be a better deal for you than any pension you take out yourself.

Activity

Take the stakeholder test by using this checklist:

A stakeholder pension could be a good choice if:

You're self-employed ☐

You're not working but can afford to pay for a pension ☐

Your employer doesn't offer a company pension scheme ☐

You don't pay into a company pension ☐

You're on a moderate income and want to top up the money you would get from a company pension ☐

LONG-TERM HEALTH

Self-invested personal pensions (SIPPs) are a type of DIY pension designed for people who want to manage their own fund by dealing with and switching their investments when they choose.

How SIPPs work

SIPPs are tax-efficient wrappers that allow you to invest in a very wide range of funds and some unregulated investments. The permitted range of investments for SIPPs include stocks and shares on the world's major stock exchanges (and a few of the minor ones, including those quoted on AIM – the Alternative Investment Market), investment trusts, unit trusts, OEICS, gilts (fixed-rate bonds issued and guaranteed by the UK government) and even commercial property.

What's the attraction?

SIPPs provide the freedom to switch out of poorly performing investments. They also offer the potential for much better returns, because policy holders can adopt a more aggressive investment strategy than large pension funds.

Are they expensive?

They often have higher charges than stakeholder and personal pensions and, for this reason, they may only be suitable for large funds (£100,000 or more) and for people who are experienced with investing. They have the same tax benefits and regulations as stakeholder and personal pension plans and they work in the same way.

LONG-TERM HEALTH

Many people relish the opportunity to manage their own pension. But most of us don't have the time, expertise or interest to do a good enough job. Remember that with a SIPP there'll be no one else to rely on if you make the wrong investment decisions.

FACT:
Depending upon the type of investments chosen, SIPPs could have less protection than with other pensions. Because the SIPP wrapper itself is not regulated by the Financial Services Authority (FSA), not all types of investment you can include within a SIPP are regulated, and so elements of your SIPP may not be protected by the Financial Services Compensation Scheme. Take this added risk into account when considering a SIPP.

Activity

Get to grips with SIPPS

- Although many of us will never get close to the sort of income needed to make SIPPs an option, it is important to know what they are and how they work if only to understand why they may not be right for you. This will ensure that you feel more confident about your pension choices when getting advice and considering your options.

- Make sure you feel comfortable with the pension options which are open to you and begin saving as soon as possible.

LONG-TERM HEALTH

Not everyone needs life assurance until they reach certain milestones in life. If you don't have children or dependants and don't own your own property then it's something you may not need to consider until later.

Activity

Know when you may need life insurance

Not everyone needs life assurance until they reach certain milestones in life.

● Do you have children or dependants?

● Do you have a mortgage which you would like paid in the event of your death?

These are the main reasons to need life cover. Do either of them apply to you? If yes, you will probably need cover.

If you do need cover, here are the basic types available.

Term assurance

Term assurance is the simplest type. It pays out if you die during the term of the policy, which can be as little as five years or as long as 30 years, and is popular for covering a large debt such as a mortgage. If you outlive the term, the policy expires and you get nothing back.

Decreasing term assurance

Decreasing term assurance, as the name suggests, decreases over time in line with the debt. Your mortgage, for instance, will gradually be paid off over 25 years and if you were to die 20 years into the mortgage, less money would be needed to settle the debt and this could be provided by the decreasing term policy.

Whole of life assurance

Whole of life assurance takes the idea a step further. It covers your entire life and, unlike term assurance, it will definitely pay out, so doubles as an investment for relatives. Because there's an inevitable payout, this cover is usually much more expensive than term assurance and the premiums are likely to increase regularly.

Rolling term assurance

Rolling term assurance is a halfway house between term and whole of life. It guarantees cover throughout your life without medical checks. There's a payout at the end of the policy, but unlike whole of life assurance the premiums are less likely to rise by as much.

Death-in-service benefit

Death-in-service benefit is the cheery name given to the financial lump sum attached to many company pension schemes. If you die while employed then these will typically pay three times your salary, which might mean that you won't need to take out life assurance. However, if you change employer, you may lose this.

Endowment

The success – or not – of endowments is linked to the stock market and this makes them risky. Along with the investment there is also life assurance which is designed to pay off the mortgage if you die during the term. Endowments are similar to term assurance in that they last for a certain period of time. But you may not want to rely on them to deliver a certain amount such as mortgage repayment.

LONG-TERM HEALTH

Because nothing in life is certain, there are various ways that you can protect yourself financially if you become too ill to work.

Income protection

Also known as permanent health insurance or PHI, this type of plan is designed to replace your salary if you can't work because of temporary illness or disability. The policy pays a monthly tax-free income until you recover – right up to retirement date if necessary.

Critical illness cover

This insurance will pay a tax-free lump sum on diagnosis of any one of a wide range of serious illnesses including certain types of cancer, heart attack, stroke or brain tumour. Critical illness policies can vary greatly in the cover they offer. As always, check the small print when you shop around.

Private medical cover

This is designed to cover the costs of private patient treatment for curable conditions that may develop after take out the private cover. It's a popular way to avoid NHS waiting lists.

Of course, you can pay for private treatment as and when you need it, but this can be very expensive and will inevitably be an added chore when you're not feeling your best. Insurance doesn't come cheap though. On average, it costs around £1,000 a year but this can vary according to the nature and extent of your plan and even where you live. Also, the cost of care in cities tends to be much higher than for rural areas. Premiums also increase as you get older and are more likely to require medical care. You may be fortunate enough to have private medical cover provided by your employer.

LONG-TERM HEALTH

Activity

Get to grips with protection and health cover

- It's good to know what these products are and how they work even if you don't need them now. It also means you can save money by only buying the cover you really need and understand.

- Check with your employer to see whether you already have cover through work. This will stop you doubling up and wasting money.

TOP TIP

- As with life cover, you may wish to consider whether you need this type of insurance if you have no commitments or dependants. If you want to take out some kind of protection, then check with your employer first to find out whether you may already have cover. Your employer may offer health or protection benefits – find out before you duplicate cover and spend money you don't need to.

LONG-TERM HEALTH

Life's too short for us all to be financial experts. Unless you decide to spend all your spare time studying finance, it's likely that you'll need – and want – to rely on an expert for financial advice at various stages in your life.

Activity

Know how advisors work and how to find one

- Some financial advisers can only recommend the products of one company or a handful of companies on a chosen panel. Financial advisers attached to high-street banks or building societies are likely to fall into this category. The alternative is to find an independent financial adviser – or IFA.

- To find an IFA, log on to www.unbiased.co.uk for a list of those nearest to your home or work. Alternatively, call 0800 085 3250 for the same information. Surf the unbiased website for more details about finding the right adviser.

Understanding IFAs

IFAs are the only type of financial advisors who can choose from all the products available in the marketplace – making sure you get the right product for your individual needs.

They're bound to the rules of the Financial Services Authority (FSA) – Britain's finance regulator. The FSA rules oblige IFAs to provide advice most suited to your personal requirements and your risk outlook. When advisors recommend financial products to you, they must explain the benefits provided, charges, flexibility, service and financial strength. In addition, when recommending a product all financial

LONG-TERM HEALTH

advisors have to provide written reasons why they think that it's right for you – this is to make sure that you're fully informed before committing yourself to anything.

Make sure you understand, and are happy with, the advice you're given before you go ahead with a financial advisor's recommendation. Don't be afraid to ask questions – that is what they're there for.

TOP TIP

- ◆ To find out more about the Financial Services Authority and its rules, log on to www.fsa.gov.uk. The site also offers consumer advice and gives you access to the public register of regulated advisors and firms. Or try the consumer helpline on 0845 606 1234.

FACT: If you're approached by someone offering financial advice, first check that they're registered with the Financial Services Authority. If they're not and you hand over money or act on their financial advice, then you won't be protected by the financial compensation system and will have to rely on the police and the courts to pursue your case if problems arise.

LONG-TERM HEALTH

Have you got a will? Or are you happy for your assets to be eaten up by tax and the government? Law Society research reveals that at least a third of UK adults don't have a will. Many people assume that, if you don't have a will, your partner will get everything. Some think you only need to arrange a will if you're very wealthy or old. But this isn't the case.

Regardless of your age and whether you're worth millions or hundreds, it makes sense to have a will so that your estate (what you leave when you die) can be processed efficiently.

Activity

Take the will quiz

Answer 'true' or 'false' to the following statements:

- A letter conveying your desires as to what happens to your property on your death constitutes a legal document.

- The surviving spouse always inherits their partner's estate, which they must use for the benefit of the family.

- Your next of kin automatically acquires your property and has a legal duty to distribute it fairly among the members of your family.

The answer to all three questions is 'false'.

Why you need a will

◆ If you're married and have any dependants then having a will means that they can be protected and your possessions can be disposed of according to your wishes.

◆ If you die without a will in England and Wales, the old-fashioned intestacy rules don't recognise unmarried partners or step-children. It can take many months before those left behind can access bank accounts, savings and even life insurance.

◆ If you're married, the situation isn't much better. Your husband or wife gets your personal possessions and a fixed amount of money. This can create havoc if the value of the home you share is more than the £125,000 limit set by the government. With the average UK house currently worth more than £160,000, your spouse would have to find the cash to make up the difference on the value of your property or face losing their home.

◆ If you're a single parent without a will, the state will decide who'll have parental responsibility for your children – this includes the possibility of making them a ward of court.

What does it cost?

A solicitor can draw up a simple will for between £60 and £100. It can be updated throughout your lifetime. Any existing will is automatically revoked upon marriage, whether it is your first or fifth marriage.

TOP TIP

◆ Making a new will after marriage will avoid the legal nightmare of intestacy.

LONG-TERM HEALTH

Owning your own car is the key to a world of independence and convenience. But it doesn't come cheap. Along with maintenance, servicing, petrol and road tax, you'll have to fork out for insurance.

Excess

Motor insurance policies usually have excess options. Excess is simply an amount of money that you commit to paying if you need to make a claim. By opting to pay, say, the first £200 of any claim, your premium will usually be slightly reduced. Most policies have a compulsory excess that's fixed at around £50 to £100, and then a voluntary excess that you can vary.

How much will it cost?

The exact cost of your cover will be calculated according to a number of factors, including your car and your profile as a driver. Car insurance is most expensive for drivers under 25 years old. But it pays to shop around as many firms specialise in certain areas of the market. And, despite all the jokes, younger women have the last laugh with car insurance as they're statistically safer drivers than men and so often get covered for up to 20 per cent less. Your postcode will also be a major factor and there's little you can do if you live in a high-risk area. But don't be tempted to lie and register you car at another address. If you do this, it automatically invalidates your insurance.

Activity

Get to grips with car insurance basics

The main insurance options may look slightly similar but the difference can be bigger than you think. Ask yourself: If your car was damaged how much would the repair bill have to be before you would want to claim on insurance? Your insurance has to be affordable but you need to weigh up whether you would prefer to shell out for fully-comprehensive insurance now or be without your car while you save up for full repairs.

There are three main categories you can choose from which determine the amount of cover provided:

Third party only

This is the minimum level of cover required by law to drive in the UK. This covers you for the cost of any claims for damage you may do to another person, vehicles or property. But you're not covered for damage, loss or theft of your own car or possessions.

Third party, fire and theft

This cover includes third party cover, and also insures your own car for damage or loss caused by fire or theft.

Comprehensive insurance

This covers you for third party, fire and theft, plus damage to your own vehicle. Because of the added risk involved, this is usually more expensive. Nevertheless, it is the most popular type of policy in the UK, accounting for over 70 per cent of policies sold.

LONG-TERM HEALTH

187

The simplest way to keep your motor insurance costs down is to shop around for a better deal. The difference between premiums (the amount you pay) for the same cover from different insurers can be huge.

Activity

Make changes that will save money

Each of the following may all make a difference to what you pay for your car insurance. How many can you tick off now? Aim to tick off as many as possible over the next few months.

- Get a no-claims discount. Expect a typical saving of 30 per cent on your next year's cover if you don't make any claims in the previous year. ☐

- Fit an alarm or immobiliser to cut premiums, but make sure it conforms to government standards. Many insurers will slice 5 per cent off a premium if the car has an insurer-approved alarm and immobiliser. Keeping your car in a locked garage used to mean a big discount but this now varies between insurers. ☐

- Restricting the drivers to yourself and one or two named others will usually be cheaper than an 'any driver' arrangement. With some insurers, this could cut the cost by up to 25 per cent. ☐

- Limit your mileage. Look for policies that offer discounts if you drive fewer than the 8,000–12,000 miles per year average. This could knock up to around 15 per cent off your premium. ☐

- Take a bigger excess than the standard £50 or £100. Doubling the excess can knock about 15 per cent off the premium.

- Pay your full premium. Many companies charge up to 10 per cent extra if you want to pay in installments.

- Shop around and buy online – most insurers offer discounts if you buy via the internet.

- Use your age. There's a remarkable drop in premiums after your 20s. Insurance companies also target the over-50s for special policies and discounted premiums. Lower rates for older drivers reflect the fact that older people make far fewer claims than average. The savings begin at 50 and reach their peak for drivers in their mid 60s. But once drivers reach 75, rates start rising sharply again.

- Use your gender. Females under 25 generally get insurance that's about 20 per cent less than males, but the picture reverses after that, with insurers charging older female drivers slightly more than older male drivers.

- Don't lie. The most common lie is to register cars as being outside London or the other high-rated metropolitan areas, either at parents or at fictitious addresses. Doing this automatically invalidates your insurance.

Sunscreen, sandals or skis aren't the only essentials for holidays. Travel insurance may not come with ice and a slice but it's an absolute must if you plan to have happy travels. The alternative is taking your chances with the medical system of a foreign country. That's the last thing most people want when they're ill or injured, let alone far from home.

Is the E111 enough?

Some countries have reciprocal arrangements with the UK and the European E111 scheme (details available from post offices) will provide emergency treatment on the continent. But the extent of the cover varies between countries and you may still have to foot the bill for medicines or an ambulance if you need them. So getting travel insurance is essential.

FACT: If you do lose anything or it gets stolen while on holiday, make sure that you get a report from the police – this is a condition of many policies, and claims often aren't covered if you haven't got a report, especially for valuables and cash. It's also helpful to keep receipts for expensive items you take away with you such as a camera.

LONG-TERM HEALTH

Activity

Know what to look for

Use this checklist when buying insurance.

- Booking your travel insurance as soon as you can after you've booked your holiday will safeguard you if the trip is cancelled or, in certain circumstances, if you're forced to cancel yourself.

- Before you sign, check that the policy limits for personal possessions claims are adequate to cover the value of the items you're taking with you – limits for baggage cover can be as low as £500 with single article limits as low as £50.

- Reading small print is never fun, particularly when you want to be thinking about bikinis and beaches. But travel insurance is notorious for unhelpful exclusions that can make a huge difference to your protection while abroad. There are some common exclusions for personal belongings cover such as glasses, bicycles and any items that are specifically listed on another policy. These will normally be covered under your household contents insurance but it may be worth checking.

- If you're planning any water or winter sports or other adventurous activities then it's essential to check the specific details of the policy before you travel to make sure you're covered.

LONG-TERM HEALTH

You may not want to be bothered with boring things such as insurance when you're excitedly planning for your much-needed holiday. But not shopping around is an easy way to waste cash.

Activity

Know how to get value for money on travel insurance

- Everywhere from the web to the supermarket offers insurance now, but prices can vary enormously so you'll get the best deal if you take the time to shop around rather than grabbing the nearest policy the day before your trip.

- You may experience hard sell from your travel agent, but for the convenience of getting it out of the way you could pay around 75 per cent more. Every year an ocean of cash totalling more than £250 million is wasted by travellers who buy their travel insurance from a tour operator or travel agent instead of finding insurance cheaper elsewhere. Do a search on the internet for the best deals.

FACT: Take care of your possessions while you're away. Your insurance cover may not apply if you haven't shown reasonable care, for example if you leave your watch unattended on the beach while you go swimming.

Save with an annual policy

If you go abroad more than once a year it's almost certainly worth taking out an annual policy. These represent much better value than buying a new policy each time and you also avoid the last-minute rush to get cover. Annual cover also means that you don't have to worry about last-minute insurance for weekends away, which are a hot spot for uninsured problems.

Annual policies are available for individuals, couples and families and can include Europe or worldwide cover. They generally provide around 30 days cover in any one year and premiums are larger according to how much time you plan to spend abroad. Insurers offer packages for 30, 60, 90 or 120 days of travel and there are deals for backpackers who plan to spend a year or more out of the country.

TOP TIP

- Find out whether the policy will provide new-for-old cover. The majority of travel insurance policies in the UK are written on an indemnity basis, which means deductions are made for wear and tear.

LONG-TERM HEALTH

Tax is possibly one of the dullest, most annoying aspects of our finances. Unfortunately, we're pretty well stuck with it and it's important to understand the basics of what you pay.

Taxable income explained

Taxable income is the money you earn that has tax deducted from it. This table shows what sort of income is liable or not liable to be taxed.

Pay As You Earn

If you're employed, employers have to deduct tax directly from your pay (this is known as PAYE or Pay As You Earn). Your tax code tells your employer how much you've earned in the current year and how much tax you've paid so far in the current tax year. This information enables them to calculate the correct amount of tax due from your next pay packet.

Liable to be taxed	Not liable to be taxed
Earnings from full- and part-time work (including tips) Earnings from any profitable hobbies (for example, making jewellery) Profits from a business or dividends from shares Jobseekers' Allowance Rent from letting rooms in a house Interest from bank, national savings or building society accounts	Student funding Scholarships Most research awards Housing benefit Allowances from parents or spouse Grant from the University Access Fund Redundancy payments (up to £30,000) Tax-free savings accounts, such as ISAs The first £4,615 of your annual earnings (known as your personal allowance)

How much?

All taxpayers have a personal allowance (£4,615 per year in 2004/5), which is the amount you're allowed to earn before you pay tax. You pay income tax on all earnings over this amount. The more you earn, the more income tax you pay.

◆ Lower rate tax (currently 10 per cent) is payable on the first £1,960 of taxable income over the personal allowance.
◆ Basic rate tax (currently 22 per cent) is payable on the next £28,540 of taxable income you earn. So you pay no tax on the first £4,615 of your annual salary, 10 per cent on the next £1,960, and a further 22 per cent on anything between £1,961 and £30,500.
◆ Beyond this, higher rate tax is charged at 40 per cent.

Activity

Get to grips with tax basics

It's important to know a little bit about tax so read through this step and you should understand the basics. Don't worry if you can't remember all the numbers – you don't need to know them by heart. Log on to the website for HM Revenue and Customs – www.hmrc.gov uk – for more information and help. Add it to your favourites so you know where to start if you have a tax question.

A tax return is a way of informing the Inland Revenue how much, if any, additional tax you owe them. In some cases, if you're very lucky, they may even owe you some money.

Most employees don't get a tax return to fill in and have their income tax deducted at source by their employers or pension providers through the PAYE system.

Tax returns are sent to directors, employees and pensioners who pay tax at the higher rate (40 per cent) and employees and pensioners with more complex tax affairs. If you're self-employed, you'll need to fill in a tax return.

If you receive a self-assessment tax return pack, it will include a step-by-step guide on how to fill in each section of your return, together with a guide on how to calculate your own tax if you want to.

Some people – mainly the self-employed – will also make two payments on account for the tax year before the return for that year is due.

FACT: If you have any additional sources of income on which you may have to pay tax, then it's up to you to declare these. If you're not sent a tax return form to complete, then that's not a reasonable excuse for failing to declare the additional income. Contact your tax office if you're unsure of what to declare for tax purposes.

Activity

Keep your paperwork in order

Everyone who pays tax should, at some stage, receive a record of the tax they've paid. You should keep the following information you receive from your employer:

- Your P45, which contains details about your pay and tax. If you leave your job during the tax year, your employer will give you form P45. You should keep part 1A of this form.

- P60, which contains details about your pay and tax. Your employer should give you this by 31 May after the end of the tax year (if you were in your job at 5 April).

- Details of your taxable expenses and benefits in kind (sometimes known as P11D details). Your employer should give you these by 6 July after the end of the tax year (if you were in your job at 5 April).

'A child of five would understand this. Send someone to fetch a child of five.' Groucho Marx, actor and comedian

Did you know that if someone can get hold of basic information such as your name, date of birth, National Insurance number, or a credit card number, they can use this to help abuse or clone your financial records or accounts, or even create a new set of documents and accounts to defraud you? Identity theft is on the increase and can carry on for months or years without the victim's knowledge.

A classic scam

In a typical identity fraud scam, the thief applies for gold and platinum cards in your name, supplying your details, but indicating a change of address for billing. Your current cards or credit lines are untouched but new accounts are set up in your name for which you'll never see the charges.

The thief then uses the cards as quickly as possible, ignoring the monthly bills and applying for more cards. The spiral of fraud can run and run, with debts piling up. The thief could even then file for bankruptcy under your name. Meanwhile, it's unlikely that you'll know anything about this, perhaps for several months.

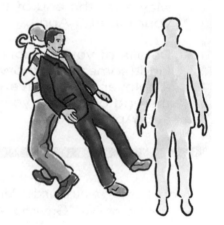

Activity

Make sure you are not vulnerable to identity theft

There are many legitimate and illegitimate ways in which personal information about you and your finances can be accessed. By being aware of them, you can avoid becoming a victim. If you don't have a shredder, it's time to think about getting one. Have a look for something small and affordable and then use it regularly to shred receipts you no longer need, junk mail or anything that contains personal information.

Here are some of the ways in which anyone can tap into your identity:

- Lost or stolen wallet/handbag. The simplest way is to lose your credit cards or have them stolen. Until they're reported lost and are cancelled, a thief can use them to spend money or as identification to get store cards.

- Anyone can send off for your birth certificate. With this, the fraudster knows your mother's maiden name.

- Public records held at the DVLA, Land Registry, Companies House and the Electoral Roll all reveal a lot of facts about you and are easy to access.

- Directory-enquiries services can provide your address and phone number unless your information is unlisted.

- A quick dip into the household rubbish in an average street provides a wealth of credit card and account numbers and statements.

- Unopened mail – perhaps in a communal hallway or sent to an old address – will provide thieves with the opportunity to take out credit cards, etc. in your name.

LONG-TERM HEALTH

Although it's easy to feel vulnerable, there are many ways to protect your identity and financial information from fraudsters.

Activity

Know how to avoid having your identity stolen

- Keep receipts from credit or debit card purchases and check them against statements. If you see something unfamiliar, tell your bank. If you don't want to keep receipts, statements and any other documents containing personal information, don't just throw them in the bin – rip them into several pieces first or, better still, use a shredder.

- Don't enter your banking details into a computer in an internet café, or if you must, make absolutely certain that you log off, and don't ask the site to remember your details. Otherwise those using the computer after you might be able to access your account. The computer might even have hacker software running on it.

- Check your credit reference files at least twice a year. More details on how your credit reference file can be useful and how to access them are given in Steps 57 to 59.

- When you move house, make sure you put a mail re-direction in place for at least a year to ensure that you can change or cancel any out-of-date contacts.

- Never reveal your PIN number to anyone.

- Use as few cards as you can. This could protect you against fraudsters who have taken to stealing just one card, or sometimes one cheque, instead of taking a whole wallet.

- Only share identity information when necessary. Never give credit card numbers over the telephone unless you've initiated the call. If someone calls claiming to be from your bank or credit card issuer then take a number and call your bank to verify their identity, even if they seem to have lots of accurate information about you or your account.

- Don't be distracted at cash machines. Look carefully at the front of the dispenser to ensure it's genuine, avoid being distracted, even if someone taps you on the shoulder or says you've dropped some money. Never let anyone see you entering your PIN at a cash machine or in shops.

- Remove your name from mailing lists as this reduces the number of commercial entities that have access to your identity information. It also reduces the amount of junk mail you get. To do this, contact the Mailing Preference Service on 0845 703 4599 or log onto www.mpsonline.org.uk.

If you suspect your financial details have been stolen, tell the police immediately. They'll inform CIFAS, the UK's fraud prevention service, which will add your name to its database.

CASE STUDY

George didn't check his bank account every day but banking online meant that he usually looked at it at least a couple of times a week. This was a big help when it came to spotting the withdrawal of £1,200 cash after his identity was stolen. His regular checks on his account prevented any further fraud and meant his bank could react very quickly to sort the situation out.

Activity

Know what to do next

- Inform lenders and the credit reference agencies of any discrepancies. Check your credit reference files.

- If you discover that an identity thief has changed the billing address on an existing credit card account, close the account.

- When you open a new account, ask for a password to be used before any inquiries or changes can be made on the account. Avoid using easily available information like your mother's maiden name, or your birthday.

- Notify your gas, electric, water and utilities providers that you've been the victim of identity theft, and alert them to the possibility that the thief may try to establish accounts using your identification information.

Will you get your money back?

Most victims of identity theft are reimbursed by banks for money stolen from them. While banks will normally refund the difference if you can prove that you didn't spend the money, cutting down on cards can help you avoid the stress of fraud. To make sure the banks do repay the funds, tell them as soon as possible when you realise that someone has taken your card.

TOP TIP

◆ For members of the public who are worried that they could be a target, CIFAS, the UK's fraud prevention service, offers a service called Protective Registration. This allows individuals to place a CIFAS protective marker against their own address, when they believe it's at risk. For example, there may have been a violent crime or burglary in which personal documents have been stolen. Find out more on the CIFAS website at www.cifas.org.uk

'Organized crime in America takes in over forty billion dollars a year and spends very little on office supplies.' Woody Allen, director and actor

LONG-TERM HEALTH

The previous steps have provided you with a huge amount of information to take in. Try not to feel overwhelmed and don't expect to remember all of it. Use this book as a reference guide for specific areas as they arise. As your lifestyle changes it will make sense to review certain steps to update your financial position.

Activity

Know how to keep tabs on your finances

- One thing that will benefit from regular reviews is your budget. You don't have to wait for any major changes in your circumstances to justify a budget review. Now you've done it once, it should be very easy to dust it off and check your progress as often as you like.

- To begin with, you may want to do this once a month because there's so much going on. If you have considerable debts and are paying them off then this is another good way to keep an eye on everything. You don't need to become obsessive about it, but once you have control over your finances it makes sense to keep hold of it.

- Apart from your budget and the ongoing affordable repayment of any debts, you'll need to keep deals under review if you want to keep saving money. Take one product at a time every couple of months – credit cards, mobile, etc.

LONG-TERM HEALTH

Life has a funny way of distracting us from all sorts of things. The chances are that you've slipped off course once or twice during this financial detox. Don't give yourself a hard time about it. If you've made progress at a slower rate or been better at some things than others, that's fine.

CASE STUDY

Don had moderate debts but was getting increasingly overdrawn and wanted to reverse this. He found the first month of change the hardest – he was worried about his debts, but also worried about cutting back on spending, and so everything associated with his attempts to improve his finances was getting him down. This is the point where many of us may give up. The difference came when pay day finally arrived and Don found he had money left over from his last pay for the first time in months. He used the difference to reduce his overdraft and started a new month feeling more positive, with plans to save even more during the next month.

TOP TIP

♦ Don't feel down if your financial picture isn't changing as quickly as you'd hoped. So much of the way we manage and spend our money is down to our lifestyle and so you may need to make important changes over some time to make a difference overall.

LONG-TERM HEALTH

Activity

Don't panic, get back on track

It's not a race. Here are some ideas that may help if you feel you need to get back on track:

- Write a list of things you've done to sort out your finances. You may be surprised at how much you've achieved. It will also help you to identify any gaps.

- Now note the areas you think you've not covered properly, not understood or not followed through.

- Revisit the relevant chapters or steps and work through them in your own time. You may need to leave a few days in between each one if you feel you're taking on too much.

- Make notes in your notebook to remind you that a chapter has been covered or write down anything still to be done.

'Money for me has only one sound: liberty.' Gabrielle 'Coco' Chanel, fashion designer

Your diary – and calendar – can be extremely helpful in keeping your money under control. After all, there are far more fun things in life than trying to remember when your mortgage deal expires or your mobile tariff needs changing. For some things – such as car tax and insurance – you'll receive reminders about a fortnight before they expire, but this doesn't happen with most financial products as the companies that provide them are happy for you to stay with them for as long as possible.

Activity

Get ideas for your own diary entries

What to check	What to do about it
Car tax – annual or bi-annual	Expect a reminder – no need to shop around.
Car insurance – annual or monthly installments	Expect a reminder but leave enough time to shop around.
Car MOT – annual	Expect a reminder and prepare for a potential bill if your car has problems.
Mortgage deal	Make a note of the expiry of your current deal and an additional note once a year to review the deal you're on anyway and shop around.
Travel insurance – annual or one trip	Be prepared to shop around.
Mobile phone	Review your tariff if you change your user habits and ask your provider if they have a better deal three or four times a year.

What to check	What to do about it
Savings accounts	Keep an eye out for better rates of interest and switch to earn more.
Budget review – monthly or as needed	Review at least twice a year and after any change in circumstances.
Debt repayment	Keep an eye on progress, interest rates and the expiry of any 0 per cent deals you're using.
Credit reference files	Review all at least once a year.
Tax return and payment deadlines	Complete if applicable (the key dates will be in your tax return).
Financial detox	Review at least once a year.
Utilities	Online calculators help you see whether you can save money – you may want to switch once a year.
Landline	Online calculators help you see whether you can save money – you may want to switch once a year.
Credit card	Make a note of the expiry of any introductory rates or the end of any 0 per cent balance transfer periods so that you can shop around.

LONG-TERM HEALTH

If only you could wave a magic wand and fix your finances in one go! The reality is that everyone's finances could benefit from a thorough spring-clean at least once a year. This will also be a chance to assess how much progress you've made in the last 12 months. It can also help you to spot and avoid potential problems or get back on track if you've slipped a little.

FINANCIAL DETOX

TO BE TAKEN
ONCE A YEAR

Activity

Detox checklist

Set out your budget, noting essential, everyday and occasional spending – this should be quick and easy if you've been keeping it under review.

Identify areas where you can cut back, including any unnecessary direct debits.

Review your spending triggers – are there new ones?

Use shopping lists if your spending needs more focus.

Prioritise any debts and review your repayment schedule – can you afford to pay off more?

Have you taken on any new or unnecessary debt?

Is your debt as cheap as it could be? Shop around for the cheapest ways to repay.

If your credit card is getting too much use, try the cash-only challenge again.

Review your bank account – is it time to switch? ☐

Review and compare your mortgage, savings accounts, phone tariffs, utilities and credit cards to ensure you're getting the best value for money. ☐

Check on your rainy-day fund – is it intact? ☐

Get hold of your credit reference files and make sure your credit history is accurate and healthy. ☐

Review your pension. ☐

Make sure your will is up to date. ☐

Think about any gaps in financial cover such as life assurance or critical illness and get professional advice from an IFA if you need it. ☐

If you're really keen, or need the extra confidence boost in the first year or two, then there's no reason why you can't do a complete or partial detox more often.

The past few months are likely to have been pretty challenging – but hopefully, it will have been worth the effort. The information, tricks and tips you've picked up will help you keep a firm grip on your finances and will support you for years to come.

Let's see how far you've come.

Activity

How are you feeling now?

	strongly agree	agree	disagree
I am more confident with my cash.	☐	☐	☐
I know there's no point hiding from my finances.	☐	☐	☐
I am more confident with money matters generally.	☐	☐	☐
I believe I can now keep my finances under control.	☐	☐	☐
I believe I can get myself out of debt.	☐	☐	☐
I believe I can avoid debt in the future.	☐	☐	☐
What I have read has demystified a lot of financial issues for me.	☐	☐	☐
I feel confident about switching financial products to get better value for money.	☐	☐	☐

	strongly agree	agree	disagree

I feel prepared for my financial future and adapting my money to changes in my circumstances.

If you scored 'agree' or 'strongly agree' throughout, then congratulate yourself on your excellent progress and success – you've come a long way and you're not likely to go back to worrying about money again.

Did you score 'disagree' for any of the statements? If you did, look back at the chapters of the book that will help you develop a better understanding or build your confidence in the areas where you feel you there may still be gaps in your knowledge.

A happy and healthy financial future

Finally, good luck with your money! Hopefully, you'll continue to find this book useful as a reference for all your financial needs. Whether you're happy with your lot or want to be a multi-millionaire, here's wishing you a very happy and healthy financial future. As film-maker Woody Allen once said, 'Money is better than poverty, if only for financial reasons.'

LONG-TERM HEALTH

Your notes

Your notes

USEFUL CONTACTS

Banking

British Bankers Association
Trade body for banks which has useful guides and information for bank customers.
www.bba.org.uk

Building Societies Association
Trade body for building societies which has useful information for customers.
www.bsa.org.uk

Mortgages

The Council of Mortgage Lenders
Trade body for lenders which has an excellent website full of useful information if you are buying a home or already own one.
www.cml.org.uk

Financial advice

The Citizens Advice Bureaux
Helps resolve legal, money and other problems by providing free information and advice from over 3,200 locations. Consult your phone directory for your local office.

Advice Now

Advicenow is an independent, not-for-profit website providing accurate, up-to-date information on rights and legal issues. It provides information on the Living Together Agreement.
www.advicenow.org.uk

Credit reference agencies

Call Credit

www.callcredit.co.uk
Consumer Services Team
Callcredit plc
PO Box 491
Leeds LS3 1WZ

Equifax

www.equifax.co.uk
Credit File Advice Centre
PO Box 1140
Bradford
BD1 5US

Experian

www.experian.com
PO Box 9000
Nottingham NG80 7WP

Energy savings

Energy Saving Trust

Encourages energy efficiency and has tips to save money whilst saving energy
www.est.org.uk

Energywatch

An independent watchdog for gas and electricity. The website contains useful information to help save energy and money.
www.energywatch.co.uk

Ofgem

Ofgem is the regulator for Britain's gas and electricity industries. Its role is to promote choice and value for all customers
www.ofgem.gov.uk

Financial services and products

Financial Services Authority

The financial regulator in the UK. Its website has lots of useful information for customers and a database to check whether a financial company or person you are dealing with has the necessary authorisation. The Consumer Information section has guides and comparison tables.
www.fsa.gov.uk
FSA Consumer Helpline: 0845 606 1234

IFA Promotion

IFAP has been running for over 17 years and promotes the benefits of independent financial advice to consumers and businesses. The site contains lots of useful information for customers and will help you find IFAs in your area and/or who specialise in a particular type of advice.
www.unbiased.co.uk
Tel: 0800 085 3250

Moneyfacts

Independent best-buy tables for dozens of financial products.
www.moneyfacts.co.uk

Debt management

National Debtline

A telephone helpline for people with debt problems in England, Wales and Scotland. The service is free, confidential and independent. Specialist advice given over the telephone is backed up with free self-help materials and guides. They may also be able to set up a free debt management plan for you.
www.nationaldebtline.co.uk
Tel: 0808 808 4000

The Consumer Credit Counselling Service

A registered charity, which assists people who are in financial difficulty by providing free, independent, impartial and realistic advice. The CCCS can assess your situation and ask creditors to freeze interest, stop penalties, accept a longer repayment period and sometimes a reduced sum.

www.cccs.co.uk

Tel: 0800 138 1111

Payplan

One of the UK's leading debt management companies and its services are free. It can help you to set up and keep to a manageable repayment plan for your debts and undertake regular reviews of your circumstances to ensure that your Payplan arrangement is still working. The arrangement then continues until all of your debts are cleared.

www.payplan.com

Tel: 0800 085 4298

The Samaritans

Provide confidential emotional support, 24 hours a day for people who are experiencing feelings of distress or despair, including those which may lead to suicide. They are there for you if you're worried about something, feel upset or confused, or you just want to talk to someone.

Tel: 08457 90 90 90

Money saving

uSwitch

A free, impartial comparison service advising how to make savings on household bills, credit cards and personal loans.

www.uswitch.com

Which?

Fights for consumers' rights in two ways. Which? campaigns to make sure consumers get treated fairly and it publishes magazines, books and websites to help people make the right choice for them. For useful comparison tables and guides:

www.which.net

www.switchwithwhich.co.uk

Money Saving Expert

The original and best money saving expert, Martin Lewis will help you save a fortune on everything imaginable. Sign up for his regular e-mails.
www.moneysavingexpert.com

Other

Unclaimed Assets Register

A unique search service that helps you find your lost assets and re-establish contact with financial institutions.
www.uar.co.uk
Tel: 0870 241 1713

National Savings and Investments

The home of government-supported savings and investments and Premium Bonds.
www.nsandi.com

Ofcom

The independent regulator and competition authority for the UK communications industries, with responsibilities across television, radio, telecommunications and wireless communications services.
www.ofcom.org.uk

Office of Fair Trading

Responsible for making markets work well for consumers by promoting and protecting consumer interests throughout the UK, while ensuring that businesses are fair and competitive. The website contains useful information and can help you avoid the latest scams.
www.oft.gov.uk

Why not try another title in the

series?

CHOKER to NON-SMOKER

0-340-91540-4

Are you **CHOKING?**
Want to *stop smoking*?

Go from **PUFFEE** to *puff-free* in 100 easy steps!

Top health journalist Nicki Defago will show you how to quit the fags forever and feel great.

How?

Each step of this 100-day program will give you all you need to drop the weed. With 'smoker profiles', interactive quizzes and motivational messages, not only will you give up and stay that way, but you'll also boost your self-esteem. Supporting you at every step, Nicki offers:

* ✳ Expert psychological tips
* ✳ Self-assessments and daily activities
* ✳ Motivational methods
* ✳ Strategies for success
* ✳ Exercises and emergency plans

Former BBC journalist **NICKI DEFAGO** has written on almost every aspect of women's health for *Eve, She* and *Red.*

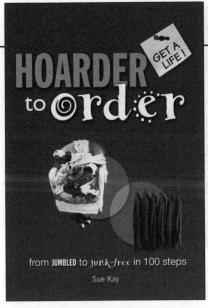

HOARDER to ORDER

0-340-90803-3

Drowning in **JUNK?**

Need to **de-clutter?**

Go from **JUMBLED** to **junk-free** in 100 easy steps!

Decluttering guru Sue Kay is here to help you say goodbye to a muddled head and messy home, and hello to a tranquil and orderly new life!

How?

In just 100 steps you'll go from cluttered to clutter-free, learning habit-changing tips to help you stay this way forever. Don't put it off any longer! Blitz that bedroom and purge that paperwork! This easy-to-follow programme includes:

* Daily activities
* Dos and don'ts
* Action plans
* Self-assessments and quizzes

Professional Organiser and leading UK declutterer, **SUE KAY's** expertise has featured on the BBC, ITV, and in numerous magazines and newspapers.

ZERO to HERO

0-340-91539-0

Go from **zero** to h:ero in 100 easy steps!

Professional confidence-boosters Christine Wilding and Stephen Palmer are on hand to help you get perceptive, powerful and positive about every aspect of your personality.

How?

Your 100-step guide to great self-esteem will give you everything you need to cope with a confidence crisis, overhauling your negative thoughts, and turning obstacles into opportunities at work, home and beyond. This practical program includes a toolbox of techniques, tactics, top tips and also features:

 ❋ Daily action plans
 ❋ Questionnaires, quizzes and tick-boxes
 ❋ Motivational stories
 ❋ Ideas and inspiration
 ❋ Key learning points
 ❋ Facts and figures

As a professional behavioural coach **CHRISTINE WILDING** and Founder and Director of the Centre for Stress Management, Professor **STEPHEN PALMER**, are among the UK's most successful confidence coaches.